CPAG'S

Housing Benefit and Council Tax Benefit Legislation

25th Edition

2012/2013

Supplement

Commentary by

***Carolyn George** MA*

***Richard Poynter** BCL, MA(Oxon), District Tribunal Judge, Upper Tribunal Judge*

***Stewart Wright** MA, Dip. Law, Barrister, Upper Tribunal Judge*

***Martin Williams** Welfare rights worker, CPAG*

*Statutory instruments up to date to **1 May 2013***

Published by CPAG, [illegible] N1 9PF

CPAG promotes action for the prevention and relief of poverty among children and families with children. To achieve this, CPAG aims to raise awareness of the causes, extent, nature and impact of poverty, and strategies for its eradication and prevention; bring about positive policy changes for families with children in poverty; and enable those eligible for income maintenance to have access to their full entitlement. If you are not already supporting us, please consider making a donation, or ask for details of our membership schemes, training courses and publications.

Published by Child Poverty Action Group
94 White Lion Street, London N1 9PF
Tel: 020 7837 7979
staff@cpag.org.uk
www.cpag.org.uk

A CIP record for this book is available from the British Library

Main work: ISBN 978 1 906076 64 1

Supplement: ISBN 978 1 906076 74 9

Child Poverty Action Group is a charity registered in England and Wales (registration number 294841) and in Scotland (registration number SC039339), and is a company limited by guarantee, registered in England (registration number 1993854). VAT number: 690 808117

Design by Devious Designs
Content management system by Konnect Soft www.konnectsoft.com
Typeset by David Lewis XML Associates Limited
Printed by CPI Group (UK) Ltd, Croydon CR0 4YY

Contents

Introduction

This Supplement to the 25th edition provides commentary on all relevant new caselaw and updates to the legislation to 1 May 2013.

Spring 2013 has witnessed more welfare reform, bringing in many changes for local authorities administering housing benefit (HB) and council tax support.

Sections 96 and 97 of the Welfare Reform Act 2012 make provision for limiting the amount of benefit certain working-age claimants can be paid if their total entitlement to welfare benefits exceeds a specified amount. This benefit cap is applied by reducing the amount of the claimant's entitlement to universal credit, or if the claimant is instead entitled to HB, by reducing the amount of that entitlement. For HB purposes, unless any of the exceptions found in the HB Regulations apply (these include if the claimant or her/his partner is currently, or has recently been, in work and if the claimant or her/his partner or dependent child or qualifying young person is receiving specified benefits), HB is reduced if the claimant's total entitlement to welfare benefits exceeds £350 (for a single claimant) or £500 (for all other claimants – eg, lone parents and couples with or without children). Note that at the time of writing, the benefit cap had only been introduced in four local authority areas in London (Bromley, Croydon, Enfield and Haringey). The benefit cap will be introduced nationally in two tranches over a 10 week period starting on 15 July 2013.

A new rent restriction scheme has been introduced for social sector tenants (eg, those with a local authority or housing association landlord), sometimes referred to as the ''bedroom tax'' or as the removal of the spare room subsidy. If the social sector scheme rules apply, and the number of bedrooms in the claimant's home exceeds the number allowed under the size criteria, the amount of her/his rent used to calculate HB is reduced. Broadly, the figure used is the claimant's contractual rent, reduced by 14 per cent if the number of bedrooms exceeds the number allowed by one, or by 25 per cent if the number of bedrooms exceeds the number allowed by two or more.

Council tax benefit was abolished by s33(1)(e) of the Welfare Reform Act 2013 as from 1 April 2013. It is replaced by localised support administered by local authorities under council tax reduction schemes. In England and Wales, local authorities may devise their own schemes or may follow a default scheme. Minimum requirements are set out in the regulations. In Scotland, there is a national scheme, administered by local authorities. The next edition of this book will include the regulations for the default schemes in England and Wales and the national scheme regulations in Scotland.

Thanks to Nicola Johnston for editing and managing the production of this book and to Mike Hatt at David Lewis XML.

Comments on this Supplement and the main work are always welcomed and can be sent to the authors via CPAG.

Carolyn George, Richard Poynter, Stewart Wright and Martin Williams

Table of cases

Table of Upper Tribunal and Commmissioners' decisions

How to use this supplement

Use the Noter-up to find out about changes to the main volume. The page numbers on the left refer to pages in the main volume. The entry opposite either states what the change is or refers to another part of this supplement where the amending legislation is set out.

For abbreviations, see the table on pxxxix of the main volume.

PART I:

NOTER-UP

General Note

The amounts for, for example, personal allowances, premiums, components, non-dependant deductions and deductions from rent are confirmed/uprated by the Social Security Benefits Uprating Order 2013 SI No 574 as from 1 April 2013.

p3 SSCBA 1992 – Abolition of CTB

Sections 123, 131 to 137 and 175 repealed in whole or in part by s147 and Part 1 of Sch 14 of the Welfare Reform Act 2012 as from 1 April 2013 in so far as they relate to the abolition of CTB.

pp6-7 SSCBA 1992 s130A – Appropriate maximum housing benefit

Subsection (3) amended and subsections (5) and (6) substituted by s69 of the Welfare Reform Act 2012 as from 27 November 2012 (for making regulations) and 1 January 2013.

[p7: At the end of the first paragraph of the General Note add:]

See p336 for a summary of the local housing allowance rent restriction scheme.

p24 SSAA 1992 – Abolition of CTB

Sections 2A, 6, 7, 110A, 110AA, 115A, 115B, 116, 116A, 121DA, 122C, 122D, 122E, 128A, 138 to 140G, 176, 182, 182B, 189 and 191 and Sch 4 (paragraphs headed "local authorities, etc") repealed in whole or in part by s147 and Part 1 of Sch 14 of the Welfare Reform Act 2012 as from 1 April 2013 in so far as they relate to the abolition of CTB.

p37 SSAA 1992 s1 – Entitlement to benefit dependent on claim

Subsections (3) and (4) amended by s91 and Sch 9 para 8 of the Welfare Reform Act 2012 as from 8 April 2013.

pp32-34 SSAA 1992 s5 – Regulations about claims for and payment of benefit

Subsection (2) amended by s91 and Sch 9 para 9 of the Welfare Reform Act 2012 as from 8 April 2013.

p37 SSAA 1992 s7 – Relationship between council tax benefit and other benefits

Subsection (3) amended by s33 and Sch 3 para 5 of the Welfare Reform Act 2012 as from 1 April 2013 in so far as it relates to the abolition of CTB.

pp47-50 SSAA 1992 s109B – Power to require information

Subsection (7) amended by s114(1) and Sch 18 para 74 of the Financial Services Act 2012 as from 1 April 2013.

pp69-71 SSAA 1992 s116 – Legal proceedings

[p71: At the end of the Analysis of subsections (2)(a) and (2)(b), but before "Subsection 7",add:]

See, generally, on the relationship between subsections (2)(a) and (2)(b), *Mohammed and Parkes v DWP* [2012] EWHC 4220 (Admin), 12 July 2012.

pp72-73 SSAA 1992 s121DA – Interpretation of Part VI

Subsection (1) amended by s91 and Sch 9 para 12 of the Welfare Reform Act 2012 as from 8 April 2013.

p97 SSAA 1992 s170 – The Social Security Advisory Committee

Definition of "relevant enactments" amended by s31 and Sch 2 para 26 of the Welfare Reform Act 2012 as from 25 February 2013.

p101 SSAA 1992 s182B – Requirement to supply information about redirection of post

Subsection (5) amended by s91 and Sch 9 para 29 of the Welfare Reform Act 2012 as from 8 April 2013.

p102 SSAA 1992 s187 – Certain benefits to be inalienable

Subsection (1) amended by s91 and Sch 9 para 31 of the Welfare Reform Act 2012 as from 8 April 2013.

pp104-106 SSAA 1992 s191 – Interpretation – general

Definition of "benefit" amended by s91 and Sch 9 para 32 of the Welfare Reform Act 2012 as from 8 April 2013.

p109 SSA 1998 – Abolition of CTB

Section 34 repealed by s147 and Part 1 of Sch 14 of the Welfare Reform Act 2012 as from 1 April 2013 in so far as it relates to the abolition of CTB.

p138 CSPSSA 2000 – Abolition of CTB

Section 68 and Sch 7 repealed by s147 and Part 1 of Sch 14 of the Welfare Reform Act 2012 as from 1 April 2013 in so far as they relate to the abolition of CTB.

p164 Welfare Reform Act 2007 – Abolition of CTB

Sections 32 to 34 repealed by s147 and Part 1 of Sch 14 of the Welfare Reform Act 2012 as from 1 April 2013 in so far as they relate to the abolition of CTB.

p170 TCEA s4 – Senior President of Tribunals

[p170: Substitute the General Note with:]

The Senior President of Tribunals is the Rt Hon Lord Justice Sullivan.

pp211-223 HB Regs reg 2 – Interpretation

Definition of "the Employment, Skills and Enterprise Scheme" and amendment to definition of "self-employment route" removed: SI 2011 No.917 was quashed by the Court of Appeal in *R v (Reilly and another) v SSWP* [2013] EWCA Civ 66, 12 February 2013.

Definition of "self-employment route" amended by reg 8 of the Jobseeker's Allowance (Schemes for Assisting Persons to Obtain Employment) Regulations 2013 SI No.276 as from 6.45 pm 12 February 2013.

Definitions of "eligible rent" and "registered housing association" amended by reg 5(2) of the Housing Benefit (Amendment) Regulations 2012 SI No.3040 as from 1 April 2013.

Definitions of "member of the armed forces away on operations" and "qualifying parent or carer" inserted by reg 2(2) of the Housing Benefit (Amendment) Regulations 2013 SI No.665 as from 1 April 2013.

Definition of "local welfare provision" inserted by reg 7(2) of the Social Security (Miscellaneous Amendments) Regulations 2013 SI No.443 as from 2 April 2013.

Definitions of "employment and support allowance" and "jobseeker's allowance" inserted by reg 2(2) of the Benefit Cap (Housing Benefit) Regulations 2012 SI No.2994 as from 15 April 2013.

Definitions of "the 2012 Act" and "personal independence payment" inserted and definition of "the benefit Acts" and "person who requires overnight care" amended by reg 8 and Sch para 36(2) of the Personal Independence Payment (Supplementary Provisions and Consequential Amendments) Regulations 2013 SI No.388 as from 8 April 2013.

Definition of "armed forces independence payment" inserted and definitions of "the benefit Acts" and "person who requires overnight care" amended by Art 7 and Sch para 34(2) of the Armed Forces and Reserve Forces Compensation Scheme (Consequential Provisions: Subordinate Legislation) Order 2013 SI No.591 as from 8 April 2013.

Definition of "contributory employment and support allowance" substituted and definition of "universal credit" inserted by reg 35(2) of the Universal Credit (Consequential, Supplementary, Incidental and Miscellaneous Provisions) Regulations 2013 SI No.630 as from 29 April 2013.

pp237-248 HB Regs reg 7 – Circumstances in which a person is or is not to be treated as occupying a dwelling as his home

Para (8)(c)(ii) amended, para (16)(c)(i) substituted and para (16A) inserted by reg 7(3) of the Social Security (Miscellaneous Amendments) Regulations 2013 SI No.443 as from 2 April 2013.

[p242: At the end of the first paragraph of the Analysis to paragraphs (1) and (2), add:]

In *MM v SSWP (IS* [2012] UKUT 358 (AAC), Judge Wikeley pointed out that a tribunal acts at its peril if it defines the relevant legal test in terms of "living at" or "permanently residing at" a property; the proper test is whether or not the claimant "normally occupies" a property as her/his home.

[p246: In the paragraph numbered (4) (starting on p245), after the sentence "This is emphasised in R(H) 4/07 ... decorating the dwelling." add:]

Judge Mesher, in *DM v London Borough of Lewisham and SSWP (HB)* [2013] UKUT 26 (AAC), rejected arguments that *R(H) 4/07* was wrongly decided and said that, subject to human rights arguments, the meaning of regulation 7(8)(c)(i) was to be regarded as settled at the level of the Upper Tribunal. He then went on to consider whether the interpretation of "adapt the dwelling" adopted in *R(H) 4/07,* and other decisions, discriminated against disabled people contrary to article 14 of the European Convention on Human Rights (the ECHR) in conjunction with article 8 (right to respect for the private and family life) and/or article 1 of Protocol 1 (protection of property). Judge Mesher decided that there was a not a difference of treatment on the ground of a personal characteristic under article 14 of the ECHR, but in any event, even on the assumption that the claimant's case under that article did not fail, the difference of treatment of the claimant was objectively and reasonably justified, so that there was no contravention of article 14.

pp272-309 HB Regs reg 10 – Persons from abroad

[p276: Second paragraph from the bottom, under heading "A note on British Citizens and the Directive", in the citation for the McCarthy case, replace "not yet reported" with the new reference "103375".]

[p279: Immediately before the final paragraph, commencing "Once someone...", add:]

In *SSWP v RR* [2013] UKUT 21 (AAC), a three-judge panel of the Upper Tribunal dealt with a case where, on the facts, the claimant, a German citizen, had entered the UK in 2006 with an offer of employment. Taking up the offer of employment was delayed initially because the job involved working from home and a lack of suitable conditions at home precluded this. Then the claimant was diagnosed with breast cancer and this caused further delays. She claimed income support at a time when the job offer still remained open to her and the claim was refused.

The three-judge panel, highlighted that Article 39 EC (now Article 45 TFEU) in addition to granting residence rights to those who are in work (as discussed thus far in this section), to seek work (an excluded right of residence for HB purposes due to para (3A)(b) and (d) of this regulation as discussed at [2.1] p293) and to remain in residence if certain conditions are met once work ceases (as discussed at [1.3], p281), also contains a distinct free movement right to move to, and reside in, a Member State for the purpose of accepting an offer of employment actually made (Article 39(3)(a) and (b)).

The Upper Tribunal commented as follows:

"41. In very many cases, a person moving to another Member State holding an offer of employment will take up that offer within a matter of days or weeks. It will often be the case, however, that a short period before actually beginning the employment will be needed while the person holding the offer sorts out the practical matters which are inherent in any relocation connected with work. It will only be in very unusual cases that a person holding a job offer will not have taken up an immediate offer of employment within three months. We choose that period for two reasons. Firstly, the Citizenship Directive gives all Union citizens an unconditional right of residence for up to three months. Secondly, the period of derogation provided by Article 24(2) of the Citizenship Directive within which there is no obligation on a host Member State to provide social assistance is also three months.

42. The case before us is one which we consider to be exceptional. Circumstances conspired to prevent the claimant from being able to take up the offer of employment actually made for a considerable period, but the offer had not been withdrawn. The possibility of taking it up was becoming more problematic when the accommodation problems were compounded by the serious health condition of the claimant. But, and we regard this as significant, the putative employer had confirmed in emails before the First-tier tribunal that the offer remained open at all material times."

It goes on to find that a person with a right of residence which exists in such a scenario does count as a worker under Directive 2004/38. As such, a person in this situation comes within para (3B)(a) of reg 10 and cannot be a person from abroad (see paras 53 to 56 of the judgment which hold that is the position for the income support provision which is equivalent to para (3B)(a) of reg 10).

Although the facts of *SSWP v RR* are clearly exceptional, the case may be of wider importance for those claiming HB in the usual period of days or weeks when they have an offer of employment which they have not yet taken up – such persons cannot be persons from abroad and thus do not need to demonstrate they are "habitually resident in fact" (see [3] at p306).

[p282: In first paragraph under heading [1.3.1], replace the text from "FMB (EEA ..." until the end of the paragraph with:]

A useful summary of the cases that concern the distinction between temporary and permanent incapacity for work is contained in the Court of Appeal's decision in *Samin v City of Westminster* [2012] EWCA Civ 1468 at paras 17 to 19. The cases show that:

1. Temporary is to be contrasted with permanent: there is no middle ground between these two terms – an incapacity is either one or the other (*SSHD v FMB* [2010] UKUT 447 (IAC), approved in *De Brito v SSHD* [2012] EWCA Civ 709). So a claimant unable to work due to illness or accident, whose incapacity is not temporary will have a permanent incapacity and may be able to benefit from Article 17 of Directive 2004/38 and come within reg 10(3B)(e) – discussed at [1.5].

2. *Samin, De Brito* and a further Court of Appeal case (*Konodyba v Royal Borough of Kensington and Chelsea* [2012] EWCA Civ 982) hold that the question of whether someone is permanently incapable is an objective one (although the claimant's views may be relevant to assessing this). The question to be asked is whether there is a realistic prospect of the person returning to work in the foreseeable future. They also highlight that the question is always whether it is the health problems of the person which must be preventing the return to work rather than some other factor.

[p284: After the last paragraph under heading [1.3.2.3] add:]

RJ v SSWP (JSA) [2011] UKUT 447 (AAC) agrees with *SSWP v JS (IS)* [2010] UKUT 240 (AAC) to the effect that a person may be self-employed despite the fact no work is coming in at present and is reported as [2012] AACR 28.

[p290: Replace the whole of the second to last paragraph commencing "In SSWP v ZA ..." with:]

On 13 February 2013, the Court of Appeal gave judgment in *Szpak v SSWP and SSHD* [2013] EWCA Civ 46. The issue was whether a registration certificate applied for after the first month of employment, operated retrospectively, once issued, such that the period of work between the end of the first month of employment and the issuance of the registration certificate was then to be regarded as for an authorised employer. The Court of Appeal unanimously held that a registration certificate, issued in these circumstances, had no such retrospective effect. The decision endorses the decision of the Upper Tribunal in *SSWP v ZA* [2009] UKUT 294 (AAC) (*Szpak* was an appeal against *MS v SSWP (JSA)* [2011] UKUT 452 (AAC), a decision following *SSWP v ZA* by the same Upper Tribunal judge who had decided that case). *SSWP v ZA* also contains an interesting observation on the burden of proof in such cases. The certificate itself does not include details of the date on which it was applied for and a claimant could not generally be expected to have kept a record. However, the DWP can readily obtain that information. Therefore, in general, it would be for the DWP (or local authority in a HB case) to obtain evidence about when the certificate was applied for, so it could be determined whether the whole of a claimant's work was for an authorised employer (where the application was made after the first month) or whether the work only had that character for the first month and then from when the certificate was issued (where the application was made outside the initial month). The judge commented (at para 73) that where the DWP (or presumably the authority) has failed to make the relevant enquiries and the relevant facts cannot be otherwise established, the matter may be determined in favour of the worker (see *Kerr* referred to on p285).

[p292: Replace the text from the last sentence on this page starting "The lawfulness of this amendment..." until immediately prior to [2.2] on the following page with:]

It may be the case that this amendment is not lawful or, at least, that there may be some circumstances in which to refuse HB to a person who has a *Zambrano* right is not lawful in European law. However, before discussing that, it is necessary to set out the post-*Zambrano* caselaw of both the ECJ and the UK courts, which has gone some way to defining more precisely exactly who can benefit from a *Zambrano* right.

In *Dereci and others* (Case C-256/11) ECR (not yet reported), the Court considered the situations of a number of litigants who were non-EU family members of Austrian nationals, living in Austria. None of these cases had facts such that the Austrian national would have to leave the EU had a right of residence not been extended to her-his non-EU family members. The Court held that, absent considerations of Article 8 ECHR, no right of residence needed to be granted to the litigants in these cases: at para 66 the Court made clear that "the denial of the genuine enjoyment of [EU citizenship rights]" only occurred where the EU family member would in practice have to leave the territory of the EU altogether.

In joined cases *O, S* (Case C-356/11) and *L* (Case C-357/11), the facts in each case were that the third-country national, with a permanent residence right under Finnish law, was the mother of a Finnish national. Both mothers then married third-country nationals with whom they went on to have a further child. These third-country national fathers were then denied a right of residence in Finland. The Court reiterated that the test in *Zambrano* was whether, in practice, the Finnish children would be forced to leave the territory of the EU if their step-fathers were not granted a right of residence in Finland. At para 47 the Court explains: "The criterion of the denial of the genuine enjoyment of the substance of the rights conferred by the status of citizen of the Union referred, in the *Ruiz Zambrano and Dereci and Others* cases, to situations characterised by the circumstances that the Union citizen had, in fact, to leave [...] the European Union as a whole." Of further interest is that the Court made clear that the answer to this question was one for the judgment of the national court/tribunal (paras 49 and 50). It went on to give some guidance on when the test may be met.

(1) The mere fact it is desirable for economic reasons or to preserve the family unit in the EU is not sufficient in itself to support the view that the EU national would have to leave the territory of the EU if a third-country national was not granted a right of residence (para 52).

(2) The fact that the third-country national for whom residence is sought does not live with the minor EU national is not decisive (para 54).

(3) There is no necessary requirement for the third-country national to be a blood relative of the minor EU national (para 55).

(4) A much more relevant factor is whether there exists a relationship of dependency between the EU citizen and the third-country national (whether legal, financial or emotional). It is this relationship that is likely to jeopardize the genuine enjoyment of EU citizenship if residence is refused (para 56).

Again the Court also notes that where no *Zambrano* right exists there must still be a consideration of Article 8 ECHR.

The most authoritative UK judgment on the application of the principles in the above cases (albeit given prior to the judgment in *O and S and L*) is *Harrison and Others v SSHD*. In this case, the Court of Appeal rejected an argument that the *Zambrano* principle could apply where an EU citizen is not forced, as a matter of substance, to follow the non-EU national out of the EU, but where the continuing residence in the EU is affected in some sense because, for example, the quality of life is diminished. The parties in that case were agreed that the main focus should be on whether "as a matter of reality the EU citizen would be obliged to give up residence in the EU if the non-EU national were to be removed from the EU" – they were divided on the residual issue of whether rights could also exist where life was made more difficult and, as stated, the Courts decided no such principle existed.

A final case worth mentioning, is *CIS 1371/2012* (neutral citation not known). This case is awaiting the decision of the Court of Appeal on whether permission should be granted. The initial date of decision in the case is prior to the 8 November 2012 amendments. The Upper Tribunal overturned a tribunal decision finding a *Zambrano* right existed because, in practice, the claimant would not leave the UK even if denied a right of residence. However, that answer must be seen in the context of the fact this claimant had an extant immigration appeal at the relevant time and thus could not have been compelled to leave the UK under domestic immigration law. The same claimant as in *CIS 1371/2012*, was unsuccessful in judicial review proceedings in which she attempted to obtain, variously, interim payments pending an appeal and lifting of suspension of payments. The claim was dismissed: *Sanneh v SSWP and HMRC*.

Overall the caselaw shows the question of whether a *Zambrano* right exists comes down to a finding of fact about whether the UK national would in practice have to leave the UK if the person seeking a right were required to leave.

Having set out the scope of the *Zambrano* right, it is worth returning to the lawfulness of the exclusion of this right from being a qualifying right of residence. It is possible following *Sanneh* that the availability of sections 17 and 20 Children's Act 1989 payments might mean that a person with a potential *Zambrano* right is not being treated unlawfully by a refusal of HB (as having these sources of support means s/he would not in practice have to leave). However, one argument not put in *Sanneh* concerns whether someone with an Article 20 right pursuant to *Zambrano* could then rely upon anti-discrimination provisions in the treaty (Article 18 TFEU) to found a right to benefit and that question will have to await future cases.

[p297: Immediately prior to the heading "Under the I(EEA) Regs 2006" add:]

Para 6(3)(a) of Schedule 4 to the I(EEA) Regs 2006, as amended from 16 July 2012, also provides that leave to remain during a period prior to accession is an essential requirement for being able to use that period towards qualifying for a permanent right of residence.

[p304: At thet end of the third complete paragraph starting "In SSWP v JS (IS) ..." add:]

DJ v SSWP (JSA) [2013] UKUT 113 (AAC) confirms that this is the correct approach. In that case the claimant had never registered her work, but was able to rely on the fact that the first month was legal work in any event, to found a *Baumbast* right.

[p305: At the end of the first complete paragraph starting "The ECJ ultimately only answered ..." add:]

In disposing of the *Punakova* and *Czop* cases on their return from the ECJ, Judge Jacobs also expresses the view that the ECJ had only dealt with the first question and that the other questions will still need to be decided (see *SSWP v Czop (IS)* [2013] UKUT 351 (AAC) and *SSWP v Punakova (IS)* [2013] UKUT 352 (AAC)).

p311 HB Regs reg 11 – Eligible housing costs

Para (1)(ab) inserted by reg 5(3) of the Housing Benefit (Amendment) Regulations 2012 SI No.3040 as from 1 April 2013.

pp316-317 HB Regs reg 12B – Eligible rent

Para (1) substituted by reg 5(4) of the Housing Benefit (Amendment) Regulations 2012 SI No.3040 as from 1 April 2013.

p319 **HB Regs new reg 12BA – Eligible rent and maximum rent (social sector)**

New reg 12BA inserted by reg 5(5) of the Housing Benefit (Amendment) Regulations 2012 SI No.3040 as from 1 April 2013.

pp320-321 **HB Regs reg 12D – Eligible rent and maximum rent (LHA)**

Para (7)(a)(iv) amended by reg 5(6) of the Housing Benefit (Amendment) Regulations 2012 SI No.3040 as from 1 April 2013.

p326 **HB Regs new reg A13 – When a maximum rent (social sector) is to be determined**

New reg A13 inserted by reg 5(7) of the Housing Benefit (Amendment) Regulations 2012 SI No.3040 as from 1 April 2013.

p326 **HB Regs new reg B13 – Determination of maximum rent (social sector)**

New reg B13 inserted by reg 5(7) of the Housing Benefit (Amendment) Regulations 2012 SI No.3040 as from 1 April 2013.

Paras (2)(b) and (5) amended and paras (6), (7) and (8) inserted by reg 2(3) of the Housing Benefit (Amendment) Regulations 2013 SI No.665 as from 1 April 2013.

pp331-332 **HB Regs reg 13C – When a maximum rent (LHA) is to be determined**

Para (3) substituted, para (4) omitted and para (6) amended by reg 3(2) of the Housing Benefit (Amendment) Regulations 2012 SI No.3040 as from 1 January 2013.

Para (2)(d) amended by reg 3(2)(a) of the Housing Benefit (Amendment) Regulations 2012 SI No.3040 as from 1 April 2013.

pp334-340 **HB Regs reg 13D – Determination of maximum rent (LHA)**

Paras (2)(c), (3) and (12) amended and paras (3A) and (3B) inserted by reg 2(4) of the Housing Benefit (Amendment) Regulations 2013 SI No.665 as from 1 April 2013.

[p336: In the General Note, at the end of the paragraph numbered (4) in the commentary headed "Summary of the scheme", add:]

Note that a challenge on the vires of the amendments made to the RO orders with effect from 2 April 2012 was unsuccessful: *R (Zacchaeus 2000 Trust) v Secretary of State for Work and Pensions* [2013] EWHC 233 (Admin), 15 February 2013.

pp340-342 **HB Regs reg 14 – Requirement to refer to rent officers**

Para (8) amended by reg 2(5) of the Housing Benefit (Amendment) Regulations 2013 SI No.665 as from 1 April 2013.

p349 **HB Regs reg 19 – Persons of prescribed description**

Para (2) amended by reg 35(3) of the Universal Credit (Consequential, Supplementary, Incidental and Miscellaneous Provisions) Regulations 2013 SI No.630 as from 29 April 2013.

pp355-359 **HB Regs reg 28 – Treatment of child care charges**

Paras (11) and (13) amended by reg 8 and Sch para 36(3) of the Personal Independence Payment (Supplementary Provisions and Consequential Amendments) Regulations 2013 SI No.388 as from 8 April 2013.

Paras (11) and (13) amended by Art 7 and Sch para 34(3) of the Armed Forces and Reserve Forces Compensation Scheme (Consequential Provisions: Subordinate Legislation) Order 2013 SI No.591 as from 8 April 2013.

Para (11) amended by reg 35(4) of the Universal Credit (Consequential, Supplementary, Incidental and Miscellaneous Provisions) Regulations 2013 SI No.630 as from 29 April 2013.

p372 HB Regs reg 30 – Average weekly earnings of self-employed earners

[p372: At the end of the analysis add:]

In *CC v Braintree District Council* [2013] UKUT 104 (AAC), Judge Mark concluded that where there has been a significant change in weekly earnings from the previous year, to simply use the previous year's earnings taking into account any downturn or upturn "is the antithesis of estimating the earnings accurately". As this is so both in the year in question and in any subsequent year, this does not lead to the same period being used twice. Judge Mark also pointed out that a period shorter than a year can be used where appropriate.

pp387-388 HB Regs reg 40 – Calculation of income other than earnings

Para (5A) amended by reg 35(5) of the Universal Credit (Consequential, Supplementary, Incidental and Miscellaneous Provisions) Regulations 2013 SI No.630 as from 29 April 2013.

pp390-393 HB Regs reg 42 – Notional income

Insertion of para (7)(cc) removed: SI 2011 No.917 was quashed by the Court of Appeal in *R (Reilly and another) v SSWP* [2013] EWCA Civ 66, 12 February 2013.

Para (7)(cc) inserted by reg 9 of the Jobseeker's Allowance (Schemes for Assisting Persons to Obtain Employment) Regulations 2013 SI No.276 as from 6.45 pm 12 February 2013.

pp401-403 HB Regs reg 49 – Notional capital

Insertion of para (4)(bc) removed: SI 2011 No.917 was quashed by the Court of Appeal in *R (Reilly and another) v SSWP* [2013] EWCA Civ 66, 12 February 2013.

Para (4)(bc) inserted by reg 10 of the Jobseeker's Allowance (Schemes for Assisting Persons to Obtain Employment) Regulations 2013 SI No.276 as from 6.45 pm 12 February 2013.

pp420-421 HB Regs reg 56 – Full-time students to be treated as not liable to make payments in respect of a dwelling

Para (2) amended by reg 35(6) of the Universal Credit (Consequential, Supplementary, Incidental and Miscellaneous Provisions) Regulations 2013 SI No.630 as from 29 April 2013.

p443 HB Regs new reg 72E – Calculation of an extended payment where the benefit cap applies

New reg 72E inserted by reg 2(3) of the Benefit Cap (Housing Benefit) Regulations 2012 SI No.2994 as from 15 April 2013.

p446 HB Regs new reg 73E – Calculation of an extended payment (qualifying contributory benefits) where the benefit cap applies

New reg 73E inserted by reg 2(4) of the Benefit Cap (Housing Benefit) Regulations 2012 SI No.2994 as from 15 April 2013.

pp446-448 HB Regs reg 74 – Non-dependant deductions

Para (7)(g) inserted by reg 2(6) of the Housing Benefit (Amendment) Regulations 2013 SI No.665 as from 1 April 2013.

Paras (6) and (9) amended by reg 8 and Sch para 36(4) of the Personal Independence Payment (Supplementary Provisions and Consequential Amendments) Regulations 2013 SI No.388 as from 8 April 2013.

Paras (6) and (9) amended by Art 7 and Sch para 34(4) of the Armed Forces and Reserve Forces Compensation Scheme (Consequential Provisions: Subordinate Legislation) Order 2013 SI No.591 as from 8 April 2013.

Para (8) substituted and para (11) inserted by reg 35(7) of the Universal Credit (Consequential, Supplementary, Incidental and Miscellaneous Provisions) Regulations 2013 SI No.630 as from 29 April 2013.

p451 HB Regs new reg 75A – Circumstances in which a benefit cap will apply

New reg 75A inserted by reg 2(5) of the Benefit Cap (Housing Benefit) Regulations 2012 SI No.2994 as from 15 April 2013.

p451 HB Regs new reg 75B – Determination of whether a benefit cap applies

New reg 75B inserted by reg 2(5) of the Benefit Cap (Housing Benefit) Regulations 2012 SI No.2994 as from 15 April 2013.

p451 HB Regs new reg 75C – Manner of calculating the amount of welfare benefits

New reg 75C inserted by reg 2(5) of the Benefit Cap (Housing Benefit) Regulations 2012 SI No.2994 as from 15 April 2013.

Para (2) substituted by reg 2(2) of the Benefit Cap (Housing Benefit) (Amendment) Regulations 2013 SI No.546 as from 15 April 2013.

p451 HB Regs new reg 75D – Reduction of housing benefit

New reg 75D inserted by reg 2(5) of the Benefit Cap (Housing Benefit) Regulations 2012 SI No.2994 as from 15 April 2013.

p451 HB Regs new reg 75E – Exception to the benefit cap: current or recent work

New reg 75E inserted by reg 2(5) of the Benefit Cap (Housing Benefit) Regulations 2012 SI No.2994 as from 15 April 2013.

p451 HB Regs new reg 75F – Exception to the benefit cap: receipt of specified benefit

New reg 75F inserted by reg 2(5) of the Benefit Cap (Housing Benefit) Regulations 2012 SI No.2994 as from 15 April 2013.

Para (1) of new reg 75F amended by reg 8 and Sch para 51 of the Personal Independence Payment (Supplementary Provisions and Consequential Amendments) Regulations 2013 SI No.388 as from 8 April 2013.

Para (1) of new reg 75F amended by Art 7 and Sch para 48 of the Armed Forces and Reserve Forces Compensation Scheme (Consequential Provisions: Subordinate Legislation) Order 2013 SI No.591 as from 8 April 2013.

Para (1) amended by reg 2(3) of the Benefit Cap (Housing Benefit) (Amendment) Regulations 2013 SI No.546 as from 15 April 2013.

p451 HB Regs new reg 75G – Interpretation

New reg 75G inserted by reg 2(5) of the Benefit Cap (Housing Benefit) Regulations 2012 SI No.2994 as from 15 April 2013.

pp453-455 HB Regs reg 79 – Date on which change of circumstances is to take effect

Para (6) amended by reg 8 and Sch para 36(5) of the Personal Independence Payment (Supplementary Provisions and Consequential Amendments) Regulations 2013 SI No.388 as from 8 April 2013.

Para (6) amended by Art 7 and Sch para 34(5) of the Armed Forces and Reserve Forces Compensation Scheme (Consequential Provisions: Subordinate Legislation) Order 2013 SI No.591 as from 8 April 2013.

pp463-471 HB Regs reg 83 – Time and manner in which claims are to be made

[p469: After the paragraph of text under heading "paragraphs 10 and 11: Advance Claims" add:]

AW v SSWP (ESA) [2013] UKUT 20 (AAC) finds that the weight of authority is that a claim is "made" on each day between the date of claim and the date of decision. Accordingly, if a claim is submitted more than 13 weeks prior to any potential entitlement arising but is not decided until 13 or less prior to that entitlement arising then an advance award can still be made. Thus when looking to see whether an advance award should have been made, it is appropriate to look at whether entitlement could have arisen at any point in the 13 weeks after the decision was given.

The judge in *AW v SSWP* also comments on the discretionary nature of the power to make an advance award: he concludes that there would in general be no reason not to exercise this discretion in a claimant's favour where the conditions are met.

[p471: After the 5th paragraph, add the following new paragraph:]

"...if a claimant simply chooses not to make a claim and then changes his mind, he does not show that he had good cause for not making it. It is for him to show in some detail why he did not make it at the start of the period for which backdating is claimed and why he continued not to make it. It is possible, as in the examples of old cases that I have given, that a tribunal could properly regard a claimant as having good cause not to claim benefit for a limited period, when he is devoting his time to making real efforts to obtain work and avoid what the claimant here has referred to as the benefits trap and in the process to avoid becoming a burden on the state or the local authority. Indeed he may be applauded for his efforts in that respect. On the other hand a person who decides not to claim benefit ought not generally to expect to be able to change his mind and have his claim backdated. Also, the greater the delay in claiming benefit, the harder it may be to show good cause. It is a matter for the tribunal to determine as a question of fact whether all the facts in the particular case amount to continuing good cause for failing to make the claim."

pp498-506 HB Regs reg 100 – Recoverable overpayments

[p505: In the Analysis under "could not ... reasonably have been expected to realise", at the end of the paragraph beginning at the bottom of p504, "In CH 2943/2007, the claimant ...", add:]

CH 2493/2007 was approved and followed in *CJ v Stratford-on-Avon District Council (HB)* [2012] UKUT 357 (AAC), where the Upper Tribunal observed "Claimants are not to be expected to be particularly numerate or familiar with either accounting practice or benefit law ... they cannot reasonably be expected to realise that they are being overpaid if that would involve them realising that a trained benefit officer using the correct information was not calculating their earnings properly" (paragraph 15), and "In judging what a claimant can reasonably have been expected to realise, it is very important to look at the case from his or her perspective."

pp510-515 HB Regs Reg 102 – Method of recovery

Para (4) amended by reg 35(8) of the Universal Credit (Consequential, Supplementary, Incidental and Miscellaneous Provisions) Regulations 2013 SI No.630 as from 29 April 2013.

[p514: Replace the whole of the Analysis under the heading "The relevant benefits" (ie, ending just before "Debit from D's rent account") with:]

The relevant benefits. The categories of benefits that are prescribed by reg 105 as being candidates for recovery differ depending on whether recovery is from benefits payable to the claimant or the claimant's partner.

For the claimant the following categories of benefit are prescribed by reg 105(1) as being candidates for recovery.

(1) Any benefit except guardian's allowance: reg 105(1)(a). These include maternity allowance, widow's benefits, retirement pension, carer's allowance, industrial injuries benefits, disability living allowance and attendance allowance. It would also include arrears of defunct benefits such as sickness, invalidity and unemployment benefit.

(2) Income support: reg 105(1)(b).

(3) Benefits payable to the claimant from other EU member states under Regulation (EEC)1408/71: reg 105(1)(c).

(4) Jobseeker's allowance, whether contribution-based or income based: reg 105(1)(d).

(5) State pension credit: reg 105(1)(e).

(6) Employment and support allowance, whether contributory or income-related: reg 105(1)(f).

(7) Personal independence payment: reg 105(1)(g).

(8) Universal credit: reg 105(1)(h).

For the claimant's partner the categories of benefit are more limited. They are prescribed by reg 105(1B) and are: income support, income-based JSA, state pension credit, income-related ESA, personal independence payment and universal credit.

p519 HB Regs reg 105 – Recovery of overpayments from prescribed benefits

Paras (1)(g) and (h) and (1B)(e) and (f) inserted by reg 33(2) of the Social Security (Overpayments and Recovery) Regulations 2013 SI No.384 as from 8 April 2013.

p520 HB Regs New reg 106A – Recovery by deduction from earnings

New reg 106A inserted by reg 33(3) of the Social Security (Overpayments and Recovery) Regulations 2013 SI No.384 as from 8 April 2013.

p522 HB Regs reg 109 – Collection of information

Para (3) amended by reg 3 and Sch 1 of the Council Tax Benefit Abolition (Consequential Provision) Regulations 2013 SI No.458 as from 1 April 2013.

pp538-542 HB Regs Sch 2 – Excluded tenancies

Para 3 amended by reg 5(8) of the Housing Benefit (Amendment) Regulations 2012 SI No.3040 as from 1 April 2013.

Paras 2(3)(g) and (4) inserted by reg 2(7) of the Housing Benefit (Amendment) Regulations 2013 SI No.665 as from 1 April 2013.

[p541: At the end of the Analysis to paragraph 3 add:]

Note that the tenancies on gypsies and travellers sites are only excluded tenancies if the landlord is a county council or a housing authority (a local authority): para (1)(b) and (c). An argument that the rules as they apply to tenancies on private sector sites were unlawful under Human Rights law was unsuccessful: *R (Knowles) v Valuation Agency, Lancashire County Council and the Secretary of State for Work and Pensions* [2013] EWHC 19 (admin), 17 January 2013.

pp547-561 HB Regs Sch 3 – Applicable amounts

Para 21 substituted and para 28 amended by reg 7(4) of the Social Security (Miscellaneous Amendments) Regulations 2013 SI No.443 as from 2 April 2013.

Paras 7, 13, 14, 15 and 16 amended by reg 8 and Sch para 36(6) of the Personal Independence Payment (Supplementary Provisions and Consequential Amendments) Regulations 2013 SI No.388 as from 8 April 2013.

Paras 7, 13, 14, 15 and 16 amended by Art 7 and Sch para 34(6) of the Armed Forces and Reserve Forces Compensation Scheme (Consequential Provisions: Subordinate Legislation) Order 2013 SI No.591 as from 8 April 2013.

Paras 21, 27 and 29 amended by reg 35(9) of the Universal Credit (Consequential, Supplementary, Incidental and Miscellaneous Provisions) Regulations 2013 SI No.630 as from 29 April 2013.

pp565-572 HB Regs Sch 4 – Sums to be disregarded in the calculation of earnings

Para 10A amended by reg 35(10) of the Universal Credit (Consequential, Supplementary, Incidental and Miscellaneous Provisions) Regulations 2013 SI No.630 as from 29 April 2013.

pp573-589 HB Regs Sch 5 – Sums to be disregarded in the calculation of income other than earnings

Insertion of para A3 removed: SI 2011 No.917 was quashed by the Court of Appeal in *R (Reilly and another) v SSWP* [2013] EWCA Civ 66, 12 February 2013.

Para A3 inserted by reg 11 of the Jobseeker's Allowance (Schemes for Assisting Persons to Obtain Employment) Regulations 2013 SI No.276 as from 6.45 pm 12 February 2013.

Para 51 amended by reg 3 and Sch 1 of the Council Tax Benefit Abolition (Consequential Provision) Regulations 2013 SI No.458 as from 1 April 2013.

Para 31A inserted and para 41 amended by reg 7(5) of the Social Security (Miscellaneous Amendments) Regulations 2013 SI No.443 as from 2 April 2013.

Para 6 amended by reg 8 and Sch para 36(7) of the Personal Independence Payment (Supplementary Provisions and Consequential Amendments) Regulations 2013 SI No.388 as from 8 April 2013.

Para 6 amended by Art 7 and Sch para 34(7) of the Armed Forces and Reserve Forces Compensation Scheme (Consequential Provisions: Subordinate Legislation) Order 2013 SI No.591 as from 8 April 2013.

Para 7 amended by reg 35(11) of the Universal Credit (Consequential, Supplementary, Incidental and Miscellaneous Provisions) Regulations 2013 SI No.630 as from 29 April 2013.

pp589-604 HB Regs Sch 6 – Capital to be disregarded

Insertion of para A3 removed: SI 2011 No.917 was quashed by the Court of Appeal in *R (Reilly and another) v SSWP* [2013] EWCA Civ 66, 12 February 2013.

Para A3 inserted by reg 12 of the Jobseeker's Allowance (Schemes for Assisting Persons to Obtain Employment) Regulations 2013 SI No.276 as from 6.45 pm 12 February 2013.

Para 20A inserted and para 37 amended by reg 7(6) of the Social Security (Miscellaneous Amendments) Regulations 2013 SI No.443 as from 2 April 2013.

Para 9 amended by reg 35(12) of the Universal Credit (Consequential, Supplementary, Incidental and Miscellaneous Provisions) Regulations 2013 SI No.630 as from 29 April 2013.

pp610-614 HB Regs Sch 10 – Former pathfinder authorities

Para 4 substituted by reg 5(9) of the Housing Benefit (Amendment) Regulations 2012 SI No.3040 as from 1 April 2013.

pp622-623 RO(HBF) Order Art 4B – Broad rental market area determinations and local housing allowance determinations

[p623: In the General Note, at the end of the the first paragraph of the commentary headed "Local housing allowance determinations", add:]

See p336 for a summary of the local housing allowance rent restriction scheme and in particular the paragraph numbered (4) for an explanation of how local housing allowances are to be determined.

p635 RO(HBF) Order Sch 2 – Size criteria

Para 1A substituted and paras 1B and 3 inserted by Art 2 of the Rent Officers (Housing Benefit Functions) (Amendment) Order 2013 SI No. 666 as from 1 April 2013.

pp636-639 RO(HBF) Order Sch 3B – Broad rental market area determinations and local housing allowance determinations

[p638: Under paragraph 2 add:]

General Note

See p336 for a summary of the local housing allowance rent restriction scheme and in particular the paragraph numbered (4) for an explanation of how local housing allowances are to be determined.

pp654-656 RO(HBF)(Scotland) Order Sch 2 – Size criteria

Para 1A substituted and paras 1B and 3 inserted by Art 3 of the Rent Officers (Housing Benefit Functions) (Amendment) Order 2013 SI No.666 as from 1 April 2013.

pp667-792 CTB Regs

Council tax benefit is abolished by s33(1)(e) of the Welfare Reform Act 2013 as from 1 April 2013. Savings and transitional provisions are provided by Arts 9 and 10 of of the Welfare Reform Act 2012 (Commencement No.8 and Savings and Transitional Provisions) Order 2013 SI No.358. Regs 69, 72, 73 and 74 CTB Regs are modified by Part 1 of Sch 5 of that order.

pp799-809 HB (SPC) Regs reg 2 – Interpretation

Definition of "registered housing association" amended by reg 6 of the Housing Benefit (Amendment) Regulations 2012 SI No.3040 as from 1 April 2013.

Definitions of "member of the armed forces away on operations" and "qualifying parent or carer" inserted by reg 3(2) of the Housing Benefit (Amendment) Regulations 2013 SI No.665 as from 1 April 2013.

Definition of "local welfare provision" inserted by reg 8(2) of the Social Security (Miscellaneous Amendments) Regulations 2013 SI No.443 as from 2 April 2013.

Definitions of "the 2012 Act" and "personal independence payment" inserted and definition of "the benefit Acts" and "person who requires overnight care" amended by reg 8 and Sch para 37(2) of the Personal Independence Payment (Supplementary Provisions and Consequential Amendments) Regulations 2013 SI No.388 as from 8 April 2013.

Definition of "armed forces independence payment" inserted and definitions of "the benefit Acts" and "person who requires overnight care" amended by Art 7 and Sch para 35(2) of the Armed Forces and Reserve Forces Compensation Scheme (Consequential Provisions: Subordinate Legislation) Order 2013 SI No.591 as from 8 April 2013.

Definition of "contributory employment and support allowance" substituted and definition of "universal credit" inserted by reg 36(2) of the Universal Credit (Consequential, Supplementary, Incidental and Miscellaneous Provisions) Regulations 2013 SI No.630 as from 29 April 2013.

pp813-816 HB(SPC) Regs reg 7 – Circumstances in which a person is or is not to be treated as occupying a dwelling as his home

Para (8)(c)(ii) amended, para (16)(c)(i) substituted and para (16A) inserted by reg 8(3) of the Social Security (Miscellaneous Amendments) Regulations 2013 SI No.443 as from 2 April 2013.

pp829-830 HB(SPC) Regs reg 13C – When a maximum rent (LHA) is to be determined

Para (3) substituted, para (4) omitted and para (6) amended by reg 4(2) of the Housing Benefit (Amendment) Regulations 2012 SI No.3040 as from 1 January 2013.

Para (2)(d) amended by reg 4(2)(a) of the Housing Benefit (Amendment) Regulations 2012 SI No.3040 as from 1 April 2013.

pp830-832 HB(SPC) Regs reg 13D – Determination of maximum rent (LHA)

Paras (2)(c), (3) and (12) amended and paras (3A) and (3B) inserted by reg 3(3) of the Housing Benefit (Amendment) Regulations 2013 SI No.665 as from 1 April 2013.

pp833-834 HB(SPC) Regs reg 14 – Requirement to refer to rent officers

Paras (8) amended by reg 3(4) of the Housing Benefit (Amendment) Regulations 2013 SI No.665 as from 1 April 2013.

p837 HB (SPC) Regs reg 19 – Persons of prescribed description

Para (2) amended by reg 36(3) of the Universal Credit (Consequential, Supplementary, Incidental and Miscellaneous Provisions) Regulations 2013 SI No.630 as from 29 April 2013.

pp843-845 HB(SPC) Regs reg 29 – Meaning of "income"

Para (1)(j)(xii) amended by reg 3 and Sch 1 of the Council Tax Benefit Abolition (Consequential Provision) Regulations 2013 SI No.458 as from 1 April 2013.

Para (1) amended by reg 8 and Sch para 37(3) of the Personal Independence Payment (Supplementary Provisions and Consequential Amendments) Regulations 2013 SI No.388 as from 8 April 2013.

Para (1) amended by Art 7 and Sch para 35(3) of the Armed Forces and Reserve Forces Compensation Scheme (Consequential Provisions: Subordinate Legislation) Order 2013 SI No.591 as from 8 April 2013.

pp847-850 HB(SPC) Regs reg 31 – Treatment of child care charges

Paras (11) and (13) amended by reg 8 and Sch para 37(4) of the Personal Independence Payment (Supplementary Provisions and Consequential Amendments) Regulations 2013 SI No.388 as from 8 April 2013.

Paras (11) and (13) amended by Art 7 and Sch para 35(4) of the Armed Forces and Reserve Forces Compensation Scheme (Consequential Provisions: Subordinate Legislation) Order 2013 SI No.591 as from 8 April 2013.

Para (11) amended by reg 36(4) of the Universal Credit (Consequential, Supplementary, Incidental and Miscellaneous Provisions) Regulations 2013 SI No.630 as from 29 April 2013.

pp871-872 HB(SPC) Regs reg 55 – Non-dependant deductions

Para (7)(g) inserted by reg 3(5) of the Housing Benefit (Amendment) Regulations 2013 SI No.665 as from 1 April 2013.

Paras (6) and (10) amended by reg 8 and Sch para 37(5) of the Personal Independence Payment (Supplementary Provisions and Consequential Amendments) Regulations 2013 SI No.388 as from 8 April 2013.

Paras (6) and (10) amended by Art 7 and Sch para 35(5) of the Armed Forces and Reserve Forces Compensation Scheme (Consequential Provisions: Subordinate Legislation) Order 2013 SI No.591 as from 8 April 2013.

Para (8) amended and para (11) inserted by reg 36(5) of the Universal Credit (Consequential, Supplementary, Incidental and Miscellaneous Provisions) Regulations 2013 SI No.630 as from 29 April 2013.

pp874-876 HB(SPC) Regs reg 59 – date on which change of circumstances is to take effect

Para (6) amended by reg 8 and Sch para 37(6) of the Personal Independence Payment (Supplementary Provisions and Consequential Amendments) Regulations 2013 SI No.388 as from 8 April 2013.

Para (6) amended by Art 7 and Sch para 35(6) of the Armed Forces and Reserve Forces Compensation Scheme (Consequential Provisions: Subordinate Legislation) Order 2013 SI No.591 as from 8 April 2013.

pp897-898 HB(SPC) Regs reg 83 – Method of recovery

Para (4) amended by reg 36(6) of the Universal Credit (Consequential, Supplementary, Incidental and Miscellaneous Provisions) Regulations 2013 SI No.630 as from 29 April 2013.

pp900-901 HB(SPC) Regs reg 86 – Recovery of overpayments from prescribed benefits

Paras (1)(g) and (h) and (1B)(e) and (f) inserted by reg 34(2) of the Social Security (Overpayments and Recovery) Regulations 2013 SI No.384 as from 8 April 2013.

p901 HB(SPC) Regs New reg 87A – Recovery by deduction from earnings

New reg 8A inserted by reg 34(3) of the Social Security (Overpayments and Recovery) Regulations 2013 SI No.384 as from 8 April 2013.

p902 HB(SPC) Regs reg 90 – Collection of information

Para (3)(a) amended by reg 3 and Sch 1 of the Council Tax Benefit Abolition (Consequential Provision) Regulations 2013 SI No.458 as from 1 April 2013.

pp334-335 HB(SPC) Regs Sch 2 – Excluded tenancies

Paras 2(f) and (4) inserted by reg 3(6) of the Housing Benefit (Amendment) Regulations 2013 SI No.665 as from 1 April 2013.

pp916-920 HB(SPC) Regs Sch 3 – Applicable amounts

Paras 5, 6, 7 and 8 amended by reg 8 and Sch para 37(7) of the Personal Independence Payment (Supplementary Provisions and Consequential Amendments) Regulations 2013 SI No.388 as from 8 April 2013.

Paras 5, 6, 7, and 8 amended by Art 7 and Sch para 35(7) of the Armed Forces and Reserve Forces Compensation Scheme (Consequential Provisions: Subordinate Legislation) Order 2013 SI No.591 as from 8 April 2013.

pp921-926 HB(SPC) Regs Sch 4 – Sums disregarded form claimant's earnings

Para 5 amended by reg 3 and Sch 1 of the Council Tax Benefit Abolition (Consequential Provision) Regulations 2013 SI No.458 as from 1 April 2013.

Para 5 amended by reg 8 and Sch para 37(8) of the Personal Independence Payment (Supplementary Provisions and Consequential Amendments) Regulations 2013 SI No.388 as from 8 April 2013.

Para 5 amended by Art 7 and Sch para 35(8) of the Armed Forces and Reserve Forces Compensation Scheme (Consequential Provisions: Subordinate Legislation) Order 2013 SI No.591 as from 8 April 2013.

Paras 5 and 5A amended by reg 36(7) of the Universal Credit (Consequential, Supplementary, Incidental and Miscellaneous Provisions) Regulations 2013 SI No.630 as from 29 April 2013.

pp921-926 HB(SPC) Regs Sch 6 – Capital to be disregarded

Para 22 amended by reg 3 and Sch 1 of the Council Tax Benefit Abolition (Consequential Provision) Regulations 2013 SI No.458 as from 1 April 2013.

Para 21 amended and para 26E inserted by reg 8(4) of the Social Security (Miscellaneous Amendments) Regulations 2013 SI No.443 as from 2 April 2013.

Para 21 amended by reg 8 and Sch para 37(9) of the Personal Independence Payment (Supplementary Provisions and Consequential Amendments) Regulations 2013 SI No.388 as from 8 April 2013.

Para 21 amended by Art 7 and Sch para 35(9) of the Armed Forces and Reserve Forces Compensation Scheme (Consequential Provisions: Subordinate Legislation) Order 2013 SI No.591 as from 8 April 2013.

Para 21 amended by reg 36(8) of the Universal Credit (Consequential, Supplementary, Incidental and Miscellaneous Provisions) Regulations 2013 SI No.630 as from 29 April 2013.

pp933-940 CTB(SPC) Regs reg 2 – Interpretation

Council tax benefit is abolished by s33(1)(e) of the Welfare Reform Act 2013 as from 1 April 2013. Savings and transitional provisions are provided by Arts 9 and 10 of of the Welfare Reform Act 2012 (Commencement No.8 and Savings and Transitional Provisions) Order 2013 SI No.358. Regs 53, 57, 58 and 59 CTB(SPC) Regs are modified by Part 2 of Sch 5 of that order.

pp1043-1045 D&A Regs reg 4 – Revision of decisions

Para (7H) inserted by reg 3(2) of the Benefit Cap (Housing Benefit) Regulations 2012 SI No.2994 as from 15 April 2013.

[p1047: At end of analysis to Paragraph (1)(c): Revision while appeal pending, add:]

KD v SSWP (DLA) [2013] UKUT 23 (AAC), at para 46, holds that the equivalent provision for SSWP administered benefits to para (1)(c) is a freestanding power to revise: it is not necessary for the decision maker to identify any error of law or mistake of fact in the original decision – thus a revision decision can be made where an appeal is pending simply on the basis that the decision maker takes a different view of the facts based on the same evidence.

pp1050-1053 D&A Regs reg 7 – Decisions superseding earlier decisions

Para (2)(r) inserted by reg 3(3) of the Benefit Cap (Housing Benefit) Regulations 2012 SI No.2994 as from 15 April 2013.

pp1056-1058 D&A Regs reg 8 – Date from which a decision superseding an earlier decision takes effect

Para (15) substituted by reg 2 of the Housing Benefit (Amendment) Regulations 2012 SI No.3040 as from 1 January 2013.

Para (14F) inserted by reg 3(4) of the Benefit Cap (Housing Benefit) Regulations 2012 SI No.2994 as from 15 April 2013.

pp1068-1070 D&A Regs reg 17 – Appeal against a decision which has been revised

[p1070: After sentence which commences "Therefore in the example given above", add:]

Although in most cases, the approach suggested above, namely to look at whether the decision overall results in more benefit entitlement as a first step in determining whether the revised decision is more advantageous, some care needs to be taken as in a limited number of cases a revision decision may be advantageous even though the claimant is not financially better off as a result. This is illustrated in *DP v Mid Suffolk DC (HB)* [2013] UKUT 93 (AAC). Here the Upper Tribunal considered a case whereby the local authority had decided no valid claim for HB had been made and that decision was appealed. The authority then revised that decision to the effect that a claim had been made. The authority asked the claimant to complete a new form as, in its view, the claim form had not been properly completed. The claimant did not do this and the authority then made a further decision to the effect that there was no valid claim on the basis that the defective claim had not been perfected. The authority argued the appeal against the first decision had lapsed as its revision decision was advantageous to the claimant. The claimant argued as he had not received any extra HB the revised decision was not more advantageous. The judge holds the authority was correct in its view: he points out that reg 7(2)(c) includes in the list of what must be considered more advantageous a decision the result of which is that "a denial of, or disqualification for the receiving of [HB] is lifted, wholly or in part". Thus, it is possible that some revisions which do not award more HB to a claimant must still be regarded as advantageous: in this case as the judge commented the "revised decision no longer denied him benefit but instead resurrected his claim and gave him the opportunity to provide the further information needed to consider it".

p1094 TP(FTT) Rules rule 17 – Withdrawal

Paras (1) and (3) amended by rule 23 of the Tribunal Procedure (Amendment) Rules 2013 SI No.477 as from 8 April 2013.

p1095 TP(FTT) Rules rule 22 – Cases in which notice of appeal is to be sent to the Tribunal

Para (1) substituted, paras (2), (3), (4), (6) and (7) amended and paras (8) and (9) inserted by rule 25 of the Tribunal Procedure (Amendment) Rules 2013 SI No.477 as from 8 April 2013.

pp1095-1096 TP(FTT) Rules rule 23 – Cases in which notice of appeal is to be sent to the decision maker

Para (1) substituted by rule 26 of the Tribunal Procedure (Amendment) Rules 2013 SI No.477 as from 8 April 2013.

pp1097-1098 TP(FTT) Rules rule 24 – Responses and replies

[p1098: Immediately before the paragraph commencing "It is unclear whether..." add:]

In *MB v Wychavon DC (HB)* [2013] UKUT 67 (AAC) there had been a long delay in preparing the appeal (the facts were not clear but it was either approximately six months or approximately one year). The Upper Tribunal comments include reference to the views of the Local Government Ombudsman to the effect that 28 days should be the time within which authorities attempt to prepare the response:

"8. [...] According to the claimant in his submissions to the First-tier Tribunal, during the period of delay Wychavon continually stated to him that they could take as long as they liked in submitting the appeal and that their internal resources were such that they had to externally source the preparation of the tribunal application. Whatever the truth of this, and Wychavon has not had the opportunity to respond to this claim, the delay by Wychavon in notifying the appeal to the tribunal was wholly unacceptable. I also note from the bundle of documents submitted by the claimant to the tribunal at the tribunal hearing that the reference to the tribunal only occurred after intervention by the claimant's MP in November 2011.

9. There is no excuse whatsoever for such delay by Wychavon. Claimants can suffer severe hardship if a claim for benefit is refused. The duty to initiate the appeal proceedings that might lead to the amelioration of that hardship is placed on the council whose decision is being appealed. Independently of any special provision in the regulations, there is a duty on them to act with reasonable speed in forwarding notification of the appeal to the tribunal. They cannot simply do it as and when they please and while some allowance may be made for temporary staff shortages or similar problems, a delay even from late December to July would be unacceptable, let alone one until the following November which is then only remedied after the local MP has intervened.

10. The Local Government Ombudsman has made it clear in *Complaint No 01/C/13400* against Scarborough BC that authorities should aim to refer all appeals to HMCTS within 28 days. As I also pointed out in CH/3497/2005, a claimant is entitled under Article 6 of the European Convention on Human Rights to have his or her appeal heard within a reasonable time, and this could be particularly important in housing benefit cases where a delay could cost a tenant his home. It is unlawful for a local authority or any other public authority to act (which includes a failure to act) in a way which is incompatible with a Convention right (Human Rights Act 1998, s.6(1), (6)). The conduct of Wychavon in this case was wholly unacceptable and inconsistent with the proper conduct of this appeal."

pp1099-1100 TP(FTT) Rules – rule 27

[p1099: Add the following paragraph after the second paragraph in the General Note:]

In *TMcG v SSWP (ESA)* [2013] UKUT 411 (AAC), the claimant attended the hearing venue on the day of the hearing. The claimant, while he was in the waiting room, was told that his appeal had been allowed and he did not need to attend. Unfortunately, although he had won his appeal, he had not achieved everything he could have done via the decision of the tribunal. The Upper Tribunal set aside the First-tier Tribunal decision on the basis the claimant had been denied a right to a hearing. The decision is a useful warning: where a tribunal has taken a preliminary view the appeal will succeed it should still ensure that the appellant goes into the tribunal room (and so the right to a hearing is respected albeit that the procedure can be brief).

p1102 TP(FTT) Rules rule 33 – Notice of decisions

Para (2) amended by rule 28 of the Tribunal Procedure (Amendment) Rules 2013 SI No.477 as from 8 April 2013.

p1103 TP(FTT) Rules rule 34 – Reasons for decisions

Para (3) amended by rule 29 of the Tribunal Procedure (Amendment) Rules 2013 SI No.477 as from 8 April 2013.

p1105 TP(FTT) Rules rule 37 – Setting aside a decision which disposes of proceedings

[p1105: Substitute the Analysis with:]

Para (2)(c) applies where the party or representative "was not present at a hearing related to the proceedings". If there has been a hearing, this condition is self-explanatory. But what if there has been no hearing because the neither party asked for one, or both asked for the appeal to be decided without a hearing? Contrary to the view expressed in the main volume, the Upper Tribunal has decided that para (2)(c) does not apply in those circumstances (see *JC v SSWP (DLA)* [2013] UKUT 171 (AAC). Judge Turnbull stated:

"13. In her submission in this appeal the Secretary of State's representative submits that Rule 37(2)(c) applies even where there has been no oral hearing because the Claimant elected for a paper hearing, and that the chairman of the First-tier Tribunal therefore went wrong in law in refusing the application to set aside on the ground which she did. The Secretary of State further submits that I should set aside the substantive decision of 18 August 2011 on the ground that it would be in the interests of justice to do so.

14 However, reg. 1(3) of the 2008 Rules provides that in the Rules "hearing" means an oral hearing and includes a hearing conducted in whole or in part by video link, telephone or other means of instantaneous two-way electronic communication." I therefore think that it is clear that I was wrong, at the time of giving permission to appeal, in stating that Rule 37(2)(c) applied. It is in my view clear that it did not apply, because there was no oral hearing. That would plainly have been so if this had been a type of case heard by a First-tier Tribunal Judge alone. In a case, such as the present, where the Tribunal comprises more than one member, there must in a sense be a hearing, but where the case is determined without any of the parties being entitled to be present, because a paper hearing has been elected for, there is in my judgment no "hearing" within Rule 37(2)(c)."

Although the decision in *JC v SSWP (DLA)* is binding on the First-tier Tribunal, the view expressed in the main volume is maintained. With respect to the judge, the point is not just whether "hearing" in rule 37(2)(c) means "oral hearing" (which, for the reasons given by the judge, it clearly does). The point is rather whether one can be "present" at an oral hearing which does not take place (which one equally clearly cannot). The salaried First-tier Tribunal judge to whom the application is referred must therefore ask her/himself: "Was the relevant party or representative present at a hearing related to the proceedings?" If no hearing has taken place, the answer to that question must be no, in which case why does the paragraph not apply?

This is not merely semantics. Interpreting para (2)(c) in the way the First-tier Tribunal is now bound to do creates an undesirable lack of flexibility in the application of the rule. Most salaried judges will have come across circumstances in which procedural injustice has occurred because a party has ill-advisedly chosen to have a decision without a hearing but in which there has been no procedural irregularity within para (2)(d). The most obvious example occurs when the appellant (whose command of English may not be perfect) accidentally ticks the wrong box on the enquiry form, but there are many others. Reading para (2)(c) as if it said "there has been a hearing related to the proceedings and a party, or a party's representative was not present at it", prevents the tribunal from doing justice in such circumstances, because there will be no ground for setting the decision aside, no matter how much it is in the interests of justice to do so.

Further, the decision in *JC v SSWP (DLA)* creates perverse incentives for appellants not to co-operate with the tribunal. An appellant who would prefer a decision without a hearing would now be well-advised not to return the enquiry form at all, rather than to return it saying that s/he did not want an oral hearing. If something subsequently goes wrong, taking the latter course of action will now prevent the tribunal from setting aside its decision. The former course of action will mean that "a document relating to the proceedings was not sent to the Tribunal at an appropriate time" so that para (2)(b) will apply.

It is suggested that adopting a broad construction of para (2)(c) carries no risks that First-tier Tribunal decisions will be set aside merely because an unsuccessful appellant who requested a decision without a hearing now regrets that choice and wants a second bite at the cherry. Before the decision can be set aside, the judge must also be satisfied that "it is in the interests of justice to do so" and the appellant's "original choice of hearing will be a factor – and sometimes the determining factor – in that decision."

p1106 TP(FTT) Rules rule 38 – Application for permission to appeal

Paras(3) and (7) amended and para (3A) inserted by rule 30 of the Tribunal Procedure (Amendment) Rules 2013 SI No.477 as from 8 April 2013.

pp1107-1109TP(FTT Rules rule 40

[p1109: At end of note, add:]

The Upper Tribunal, sitting as a three judge panel, delivered a further judgment on the proper use of the review procedure, and in particular, the power to amend reasons, in *JS v SSWP (DLA)* [2013] UKUT 100 (AAC). The Upper Tribunal holds (para 45) that the power should only be used in cases which properly fulfil its purpose (avoiding unnecessary appeals while still allowing the tribunal to give the actual reasons for the decision: para 40 to 42) and in a way which minimises the risks of unfairness, or its perception, that attends its use (particularly the risk that the amended reasons will be justification or defence of the decision rather than reasons for it). Although the Upper Tribunal declined to give an exhaustive list of when those principles should result in the power to amend being exercised, it does give a useful indication at paras 47 to 50 of examples at either end of the spectrum:

"47. A clear example of a permissible amendment would be an issue that had been expressly raised on the appeal and explored at the hearing, but not mentioned in the written reasons. In such a case, it would be clear that part of the tribunal's reasoning was missing by oversight, and there would be no danger of the judge writing a justification by reference to the grounds of appeal.

48. Another example of a permissible amendment would be a passage that was ambiguous or otherwise unclear in what it was saying. In such a case, it would be clear that something had gone wrong with the composition of the reasons and there would be limited scope for the judge to drift away from the task of explaining what the passage meant.

49. In both these examples, amending the reasons would not undermine the parties' confidence in the judicial decision-making process and the finality of decisions. The amendment would be directed to and might avoid the need for an appeal.

50. At the other extreme, an example of an impermissible amendment would be a passage that gave a poor explanation of a tribunal's analysis of a piece of evidence. In such a case, it would not be self-evident that something had gone wrong, and there would be an effectively unavoidable risk that the judge, in seeking to bolster the reasons already given, would drift into supplementing the tribunal's actual reasons and, perhaps, into justification. And both those dangers would undermine confidence in the judicial decision-making process and in the finality of decisions. It is unlikely that the amendment would avoid the desire to appeal.

51. In our judgment, it is likely that many inadequacies identified in a tribunal's reasons will be at or towards this end of the spectrum and so not appropriate for amendment."

The Upper Tribunal goes on to give detailed guidance about how procedurally the power should be exercised, including noting that where the judge conducting the review is not the judge who dealt with the case (who is being asked to amend the reasons), then in general the latter judge should not be shown the application for permission to appeal.

p1110 TP(FTT) Rules Sch 1– Time limit for providing notices of appeal to the decision maker

Heading and second column of Schedule amended by rule 31 of the Tribunal Procedure (Amendment) Rules 2013 SI No.477 as from 8 April 2013.

pp1096-1097 Qualifications for Appointment of Members to the First-tier Tribunal and Upper Tribunal Order 2008 Art 2

Para (2)(n) inserted by Art 3 of the Qualifications for Appointment of Members to the First-tier Tribunal and Upper Tribunal (Amendment) Order 2012 SI No. 897 as from 16 April 2012.

pp1118-1110 TP(UT) Rules rule 10 – Orders for costs

Paras (3), (6) and (8) amended and para (10) inserted by rules 50 to 53 of the Tribunal Procedure (Amendment) Rules 2013 SI No.477 as from 1 April 2013.

p1123 TP(UT) Rules rule 17 – Withdrawal

Paras (1) and (5) amended by rule 54 of the Tribunal Procedure (Amendment) Rules 2013 SI No.477 as from 1 April 2013.

p1123 TP(UT) Rules rule 18 – Notice of funding of legal services

Para (a)(i) amended by rule 55 of the Tribunal Procedure (Amendment) Rules 2013 SI No.477 as from 1 April 2013.

p1133 TP(UT) Rules rule 40 – Decisions

Para (2) amended by rule 56 of the Tribunal Procedure (Amendment) Rules 2013 SI No.477 as from 1 April 2013.

pp1141-1142 FTT and UT (Composition of Tribunal) Order 2008 Art 8 – Tribunal consisting of two or more members

[p1141: For "3 November 2008" substitute "1 February 2013" and replace the complete practice statement with:]

1. In this Practice Statement;

a. "the 2008 Order" means the First-tier Tribunal and Upper Tribunal (Composition of Tribunal) Order 2008;

b. "the Qualifications Order" means the Qualifications for Appointment of Members to the First-tier Tribunal and Upper Tribunal Order 2008;

c. "the 2008 Rules" means the Tribunal Procedure (First-tier Tribunal) (Social Entitlement Chamber) Rules 2008;

d. "social security and child support case" has the meaning given in rule 1(3) of the 2008 Rules.

2. In exercise of the powers conferred by the 2008 Order the Senior President of Tribunals makes the following determinations and supplementary provision:

3. The number of members of the Tribunal must not exceed three.

4. Where the appeal relates to an attendance allowance or a disability living allowance under Part III of the Social Security Contributions and Benefits Act 1992, the Tribunal must, subject to paragraphs 8 to 13, consist of a Tribunal Judge, a Tribunal Member who is a registered medical practitioner, and a Tribunal Member who has a disability qualification as set out in article 2(3) of the Qualifications Order.

5. Where –

a. the appeal involves the personal capability assessment, as defined in regulation 2(1) of the Social Security (Incapacity for Work)(General) Regulations 1995;

b. the appeal involves the limited capability for work assessment, as defined in regulation 2(1) of the Employment and Support Allowance Regulations 2008;

c. the appeal involves the determination of limited capability for work-related activity within the meaning of regulations 34 and 35 of the Employment and Support Allowance Regulations 2008;

d. the appeal is made under section 11(1)(b) of the Social Security (Recovery of Benefits) Act 1997;

e. the appeal raises issues relating to severe disablement allowance under section 68 of the Social Security Contributions and Benefits Act 1992 or industrial injuries benefit under Part V of that Act (except for an appeal where the only issue is whether there should be a declaration of an industrial accident under section 29(2) of the Social Security Act 1998);

f. the appeal is made under section 4 of the Vaccine Damage Payments Act 1979;

g. the appeal is against a certificate of NHS charges under section 157(1) of the Health and Social Care (Community Health and Standards) Act 2003;

h. the appeal arises under Part IV of the Child Maintenance and Other Payments Act 2008;

the Tribunal must, subject to paragraphs 7 to 14, consist of a Tribunal Judge and a Tribunal Member who is a registered medical practitioner.

6. In any other case the Tribunal must consist of a Tribunal Judge.

7. The Chamber President may determine that the Tribunal constituted under paragraph 5 or 6 must also include –

a. a Tribunal Member who is an accountant within the meaning of Article 2(i) of the Qualifications Order, where the appeal may require the examination of financial accounts;

b. an additional Member who is a registered medical practitioner, where the complexity of the medical issues in the appeal so demands;

c. such an additional Tribunal Judge or Member as he considers appropriate for the purposes of providing further experience for that additional Judge or Member or for assisting the Chamber President in the monitoring of standards of decision-making.

8. Where the Chamber President considers, in a particular case, that a matter that would otherwise be decided in accordance with paragraphs 4 or 5 only raises questions of law and the expertise of any of the other members is not necessary to decide the matter, the Chamber President may direct that the Tribunal must consist of a Tribunal Judge, or a Tribunal Judge and any Tribunal Member whose experience and qualifications are necessary to decide the matter.

9. The powers of the Chamber President referred to in paragraphs 7, 8, 10 and 12 may be delegated to a Regional Tribunal Judge and those referred to in paragraphs 7, 8 and 12 may be delegated to a District Tribunal Judge.

10. A decision, including a decision to give a direction or make an order, made under, or in accordance with, rules 5 to 9, 11, 14 to 19, 25(3), 30, 32, 36, 37 or 41 of the 2008 Rules may be made by a Tribunal Judge, except that a decision made under, or in accordance, with rule 7(3) or rule 5(3)(b) to treat a case as a lead case (whether in accordance with rule 18 (lead cases) or otherwise) of the 2008 Rules must be made by the Chamber President.

11. The determination of an application for permission to appeal under rule 38 of the 2008 Rules and the exercise of the power of review under section 9 of the Tribunals, Courts and Enforcement Act 2007 must be carried out –

a. where the Judge who constituted or was a member of the Tribunal that made the decision was a fee-paid Judge, by a Judge who holds or has held salaried judicial office; or

b. where the Judge who constituted or was a member of the Tribunal that made the decision was a salaried Judge, by that Judge or, if it would be impracticable or cause undue delay, by another salaried Tribunal Judge, save that, where the decision is set aside under section 9(4)(c) of the Act, the matter may only be re-decided under section 9(5)(a) by a Tribunal composed in accordance with paragraph 4, 5 or 6 above.

12. Where the Tribunal consists of a Tribunal Judge and one or two Tribunal Members, the Tribunal Judge shall be the presiding member. Where the Tribunal comprises more than one Tribunal Judge, the Chamber President must select the presiding member. The presiding member may regulate the procedure of the Tribunal.

13. Under rule 34(2) of the 2008 Rules it will be for the presiding member to give any written statement of reasons.

14. In rule 25(2) (Medical and physical examination in appeals under section 12 of the Social Security Act 1998) of the 2008 Rules "an appropriate member" of the Tribunal is a Tribunal Member who is a registered medical practitioner.

SIR JEREMY SULLIVAN, SENIOR PRESIDENT OF TRIBUNALS
1 February 2013

The effect is that HB/CTB appeals will almost always be heard by a single tribunal judge.

For a discussion of the legal issues arising out of the Practice Statement, see *MB and others v SSWP (ESA and DLA)* [2013] UKUT 0111 (AAC).

pp1150-1151 Local Government Finance Act 1992 s13 – Reduced amounts

Subsection (10) amended by reg 8 and Sch para 7(2) of the Personal Independence Payment (Supplementary Provisions and Consequential Amendments) Regulations 2013 SI No.388 as from 8 April 2013.

pp1153-1154 Local Government Finance Act 1992 s80 – Reduced amounts

Subsection (10) amended by reg 8 and Sch para 7(3) of the Personal Independence Payment (Supplementary Provisions and Consequential Amendments) Regulations 2013 SI No.388 as from 8 April 2013.

p1159 Note Welfare Reform and Pensions Act 1999 – Abolition of CTB

Sections 57 and 58 repealed in whole or in part by s147 and Part 1 of Sch 14 of the Welfare Reform Act 2012 as from 1 April 2013 in so far as they relate to the abolition of CTB.

pp1159-1160 Welfare Reform and Pensions Act 1999 s72 – Supply of information for certain purposes

Para (3) amended by reg 15 of the Universal Credit (Consequential, Supplementary, Incidental and Miscellaneous Provisions) Regulations 2013 SI No.630 as from 29 April 2013.

p1165 Immigration and Asylum Act 1998 – Abolition of CTB

Section 115(1)(k) repealed by s147 and Part 1 of Sch 14 of the Welfare Reform Act 2012 as from 1 April 2013.

p1171 Social Security Fraud Act 2001 – Abolition of CTB

Sections 6B and 9 repealed in whole or in part by s147 and Part 1 of Sch 14 of the Welfare Reform Act 2012 as from 1 April 2013 in so far as they relate to the abolition of CTB.

p1173 Social Security Fraud Act 2001 s6A – Meaning of "disqualifying benefit" and "sanctionable benefit" for purposes of sections 6B and 7

Definition of "disqualifying benefit" amended by s31 and Sch 2 para 57 of the Welfare Reform Act 2012 as from 25 February 2013.

Subsection (1) amended by s117 of the Welfare Reform Act 2013 as from 1 and 6 April 2013.

Definitions of "disqualifying benefit" and "sanctionable benefit" amended by s91 and Sch 9 para 46 of the Welfare Reform Act 2012 as from 8 April 2013.

pp1173-1174 Social Security Fraud Act 2001 s6B – Loss of benefit in case of conviction, penalty or caution for benefit offences

Subsection (5) amended by s31 and Sch 2 para 58(2) of the Welfare Reform Act 2012 as from 25 February 2013.

Subsection (11) amended and subsections (11A), (14) and (15) inserted by s118(3)-(6) of the Welfare Reform Act 2012 as from 1 April 2013.

Subsection (3) amended by s119(2) of the Welfare Reform Act 2012 as from 1 April 2013.

Subsection (5) amended by s33 and Sch 3 para 16 of the Welfare Reform Act 2012 as from 1 April 2013 in so far as it relates to the abolition of CTB.

pp1177-1179 Social Security Fraud Act 2001 s7 – Loss of benefit for second or subsequent conviction of benefit offence

Subsection (3) amended by s31 and Sch 2 para 59(2) of the Welfare Reform Act 2012 as from 25 February 2013.

Subsection (1A) inserted by s118(7) of the Welfare Reform Act 2012 as from 1 April 2013.

Heading and subsections (1), (6) and (8) amended and subsections (6A), (7A), (7B), (8A), (10A) and (10B) inserted by s119(3)-(11) of the Welfare Reform Act 2012 as from 1 April 2013.

Subsection (2) amended by s33 and Sch 3 para 17 of the Welfare Reform Act 2012 as from 1 April 2013 in so far as it relates to the abolition of CTB.

pp1180-1181 Social Security Fraud Act 2001 s9 – Effect of offence on benefits of offender's family

Subsections (1) and (2) amended by s31 and Sch 2 para 61(2) and (3) of the Welfare Reform Act 2012 as from 25 February 2013.

p1182 Social Security Fraud Act 2001 s10 – Power to supplement and mitigate loss of benefit provisions

Subsection (3) amended by s31 and Sch 2 para 62 of the Welfare Reform Act 2012 as from 25 February 2013.

Subsection (3) amended by s91 and Sch 9 para 47 of the Welfare Reform Act 2012 as from 8 April 2013.

pp1182-1183 Social Security Fraud Act 2001 s11 – Loss of benefit regulations

Subsection (3) amended by s31 and Sch 2 para 63(3) of the Welfare Reform Act 2012 as from 25 February 2013.

Heading and subsections (3) and (4) amended by s118(8) of the Welfare Reform Act 2012 as from 1 April 2013.

Subsection (3) amended by s119(12) of the Welfare Reform Act 2012 as from 1 April 2013.

Subsection (3) amended by s33 and Sch 3 para 18 of the Welfare Reform Act 2012 as from 1 April 2013 in so far as it relates to the abolition of CTB.

p1189 Welfare Reform Act 2012 – Abolition of CTB

Section 130(7)(c) repealed by s147 and Part 1 of Sch 14 of the Welfare Reform Act 2012 as from 1 April 2013 in so far as it relates to the abolition of CTB.

p1189 Welfare Reform Act 2012 s96 – Benefit cap

s96 of the Welfare Reform Act 2012: Commencement 27.11.12 for making regulations; 15.4.13 for all other purposes.

p1189 Welfare Reform Act 2012 s97 – Benefit cap: supplementary

s97 of the Welfare Reform Act 2012: Commencement of subs (1)-(4) 27.11.12; of subs(5) and (6) 15.4.13.

pp1189-1190 Welfare Reform Act 2012 s97– Benefit cap: supplementary

Subsection (4)(a) amended by the Health and Social Care Act 2012 (Consequential Amendments) Order 2013 SI No.594 as from 1 April 2013.

p1218 DFA Regs reg 2 – Discretionary housing payments

Para (1)(a) and (b) amended and para (3)(a) deleted by reg 3 and Sch 1 of the Council Tax Benefit Abolition (Consequential Provision) Regulations 2013 SI No.458 as from 1 April 2013.

p1217 DFA Regs reg 3 – Circumstances in which discretionary housing payments may be made

Subpara (c) amended and sunparas (d) and (e) deleted by reg 3 and Sch 1 of the Council Tax Benefit Abolition (Consequential Provision) Regulations 2013 SI No.458 as from 1 April 2013.

p1219 DFA Regs reg 4 – Limit on the amount of the discretionary housing payment which may be made

Subpara (a) amended and subpara (b) deleted by reg 3 and Sch 1 of the Council Tax Benefit Abolition (Consequential Provision) Regulations 2013 SI No.458 as from 1 April 2013.

p1220 DFA Regs reg 5 – Period for, or in respect of which, discretionary housing payments may be made

Para (2) amended by reg 3 and Sch 1 of the Council Tax Benefit Abolition (Consequential Provision) Regulations 2013 SI No.458 as from 1 April 2013.

p1220 DFA Regs reg 6 – Form, manner and procedure for claims

Paras (1) and (2) amended by reg 3 and Sch 1 of the Council Tax Benefit Abolition (Consequential Provision) Regulations 2013 SI No.458 as from 1 April 2013.

pp1224-1225 Social Security (Loss of Benefit) Regulations 2001 reg 1 – Citation, commencement and interpretation

Definitions of "the 2007 Act", "the 2012 Act", "the Administration Act", "the ESA Regulations", "the UC Regulations", "assessment period", "income-based jobseeker's allowance", "income-related employment and support allowance", "joint claimant", "personal independence payment", and "universal credit" inserted by reg 3 of the Social Security (Loss of Benefit) (Amendment) Regulations 2013 SI No.385 as from 1, 8 and 29 April 2013.

Definition of "armed forces independence payment" inserted by Art 7 and Sch para 22(2) of the Armed Forces and Reserve Forces Compensation Scheme (Consequential Provisions: Subordinate Legislation) Order 2013 SI No.591 as from 8 April 2013.

pp1225-1226 Social Security (Loss of Benefit) Regulations 2001 reg 1A – Disqualification period: section 6B(11) of the Act

Paras (2), (6) and (7) amended and paras (5A), (6A) and (6B) inserted by reg 4 of the Social Security (Loss of Benefit) (Amendment) Regulations 2013 SI No.385 as from 1 and 29 April 2013.

pp1226-1227 Social Security (Loss of Benefit) Regulations 2001 reg 2 – Disqualification period: section 7(6) of the Act

Paras (2), (6) and (7) amended and paras (5A), (6A), (6B) and (8) inserted by reg 5 of the Social Security (Loss of Benefit) (Amendment) Regulations 2013 SI No.385 as from 1 and 29 April 2013.

p1227 Social Security (Loss of Benefit) Regulations 2001 New reg 2A – Prescribed offences: section 6B(14)(b) of the Act

New reg 2A inserted by reg 6 of the Social Security (Loss of Benefit) (Amendment) Regulations 2013 SI No.385as from 1 April 2013.

pp1283-1284 Social Security (Information-sharing in Relation to Welfare Services Etc) Regs 2012 reg 2 – Interpretation

Definitions of "local welfare provision" and "universal credit" inserted and definition of "troubled families programme" amended by reg 3(2) of the Social Security (Information-sharing in Relation to Welfare Services Etc) Amendment and Prescribed Bodies Regulations 2013 SI No.454 as from 1 April 2013.

pp1284-1285 Social Security (Information-sharing in Relation to Welfare Services Etc) Regs 2012 reg 4 – Prescribed benefits

Para (e) amended by reg 8 and Sch para 48 of the Personal Independence Payment (Supplementary Provisions and Consequential Amendments) Regulations 2013 SI No.388 as from 8 April 2013.

p1285 **Social Security (Information-sharing in Relation to Welfare Services Etc) Regs 2012 reg 5 – Supply of relevant information by the Secretary of State**

Para (1) amended by reg 3(3) of the Social Security (Information-sharing in Relation to Welfare Services Etc) Amendment and Prescribed Bodies Regulations 2013 SI No.454 as from 1 April 2013.

pp1285-1286 **Social Security (Information-sharing in Relation to Welfare Services Etc) Regs 2012 reg 6 – Holding purposes**

Para (1) amended by reg 3 and Sch 1 of the Council Tax Benefit Abolition (Consequential Provision) Regulations 2013 SI No.458 as from 1 April 2013.

Para (1) amended by reg 3(4) of the Social Security (Information-sharing in Relation to Welfare Services Etc) Amendment and Prescribed Bodies Regulations 2013 SI No.454 as from 1 April 2013.

p1287 **Social Security (Information-sharing in Relation to Welfare Services Etc) Regs 2012 reg 7 – Using purposes connected with welfare services and housing benefit**

Paras (1) and (3) amended by reg 3(5) of the Social Security (Information-sharing in Relation to Welfare Services Etc) Amendment and Prescribed Bodies Regulations 2013 SI No.454 as from 1 April 2013.

p1287 **Social Security (Information-sharing in Relation to Welfare Services Etc) Regs 2012 reg 8 – Using purposes connected with the troubled families programme**

Heading and paras (1), (3) and (4) amended and para (5) inserted by reg 3(6) of the Social Security (Information-sharing in Relation to Welfare Services Etc) Amendment and Prescribed Bodies Regulations 2013 SI No.454 as from 1 April 2013.

p1287 **Social Security (Information-sharing in Relation to Welfare Services Etc) Regs 2012 reg 9 – Using purposes connected with under-occupation and benefit cap**

Paras (1) and (3) amended by reg 3(7) and (8) of the Social Security (Information-sharing in Relation to Welfare Services Etc) Amendment and Prescribed Bodies Regulations 2013 SI No.454 as from 1 April 2013.

p1288 **Social Security (Information-sharing in Relation to Welfare Services Etc) Regs 2012 new reg 9B – Using purposes connected with local welfare provision**

New reg 9B inserted by reg 3(9) of the Social Security (Information-sharing in Relation to Welfare Services Etc) Amendment and Prescribed Bodies Regulations 2013 SI No.454 as from 1 April 2013.

p1288 **Social Security (Information-sharing in Relation to Welfare Services Etc) Regs 2012 reg 10 – Qualifying persons**

Reg 10 substituted by reg 3(10) of the Social Security (Information-sharing in Relation to Welfare Services Etc) Amendment and Prescribed Bodies Regulations 2013 SI No.454 as from 1 April 2013.

p1288 **Social Security (Information-sharing in Relation to Welfare Services Etc) Regs 2012 reg 11 – Excepted matters**

Para (1) amended and para (1A) inserted by by reg 3(11 and (12)) of the Social Security (Information-sharing in Relation to Welfare Services Etc) Amendment and Prescribed Bodies Regulations 2013 SI No.454 as from 1 April 2013.

p1288 **Social Security (Information-sharing in Relation to Welfare Services Etc) Regs 2012 new reg 16 – Holding purposes**

New reg 16 inserted by reg 3(16) of the Social Security (Information-sharing in Relation to Welfare Services Etc) Amendment and Prescribed Bodies Regulations 2013 SI No.454 as from 1 April 2013.

p1288 Social Security (Information-sharing in Relation to Welfare Services Etc) Regs 2012 new reg 17 – Prescribed purposes relating to a relevant social security benefit

New reg 17 inserted by reg 3(16) of the Social Security (Information-sharing in Relation to Welfare Services Etc) Amendment and Prescribed Bodies Regulations 2013 SI No.454 as from 1 April 2013.

p1290 The Social Security (Overpayments and Recovery) Regulations 2013

Part 6 and Schedules 1 and 2 of the Social Security (Overpayments and Recovery) Regulations 2013 SI No.384 added as from 8 April 2013.

Online The Income-related Benefits (Subsidy to Authorities) Order 1998

Amended by the Income-related Benefits (Subsidy to Authorities) (Temporary Accommodation) Amendment Order 2013 SI No.266 retrospectively from 1 April 2011 and 1 April 2012.

PART II:

PRIMARY LEGISLATION

Supplementary and consequential amendments

31. Schedule 2 contains supplementary and consequential amendments.

Commencement 25.2.13 and 1.4.13.

Abolition of benefits

33.–(1) The following benefits are abolished–

(e) council tax benefit under section 131 of that Act;

(3) Schedule 3 contains consequential amendments.

Commencement 1.4.13

Housing benefit: determination of appropriate maximum

69.–(1) Section 130A of the Social Security Contributions and Benefits Act 1992 (appropriate maximum housing benefit) is amended as follows.

(2) In subsection (3), for "The regulations may provide" there is substituted "The provision which may be made by the regulations includes provision".

(3) For subsections (5) and (6) there is substituted–

"(5) The regulations may, for the purpose of determining the AMHB, provide for the amount of the liability mentioned in section 130(1)(a) above to be taken to be an amount other than the actual amount of that liability (and, without prejudice to the generality of this subsection, may provide for it to be taken to be the amount of a rent officer determination).

(6) The regulations may, for that purpose, make provision for determining the amount of liability under section 130(1)(a) above which a person is treated as having by virtue of regulations under section 137(2)(j) below (and, without prejudice to the generality of this subsection, may provide for that amount to be the amount of a rent officer determination)."

(4) *[Omitted]*

Commencement (27.11.12 for making regulations; 1.1.13 for all other purposes)

Amendments

91. Schedule 9 contains amendments relating to this Part.

Commencement 8.4.13

Benefit cap

96.–(1) Regulations may provide for a benefit cap to be applied to the welfare benefits to which a single person or couple is entitled.

(2) For the purposes of this section, applying a benefit cap to welfare benefits means securing that, where a single person's or couple's total entitlement to welfare benefits in respect of the reference period exceeds the relevant amount, their entitlement to welfare benefits in respect of any period of the same duration as the reference period is reduced by an amount up to or equalling the excess.

(3) In subsection (2) the "reference period" means a period of a prescribed duration.

(4) Regulations under this section may in particular–

(a) make provision as to the manner in which total entitlement to welfare benefits for any period, or the amount of any reduction, is to be determined;

(b) make provision as to the welfare benefit or benefits from which a reduction is to be made;

(c) provide for exceptions to the application of the benefit cap;

(d) make provision as to the intervals at which the benefit cap is to be applied;
(e) make provision as to the relationship between application of the benefit cap and any other reduction in respect of a welfare benefit;
(f) provide that where in consequence of a change in the relevant amount, entitlement to a welfare benefit increases or decreases, that increase or decrease has effect without any further decision of the Secretary of State;
(g) make supplementary and consequential provision.

(5) In this section the "relevant amount" is an amount specified in regulations.

(6) The amount specified under subsection (5) is to be determined by reference to estimated average earnings.

(7) In this section "estimated average earnings" means the amount which, in the opinion of the Secretary of State, represents at any time the average weekly earnings of a working household in Great Britain after deductions in respect of tax and national insurance contributions.

(8) The Secretary of State may estimate such earnings in such manner as the Secretary of State thinks fit.

(9) Regulations under this section may not provide for any reduction to be made from a welfare benefit–

(a) provision for which is within the legislative competence of the Scottish Parliament;
(b) provision for which is within the legislative competence of the National Assembly for Wales;
(c) provision for which is made by the Welsh Ministers, the First Minister for Wales or the Counsel General to the Welsh Assembly Government.

(10) In this section–

"couple" means two persons of a prescribed description;
"prescribed" means prescribed in regulations;
"regulations" means regulations made by the Secretary of State;
"single person" means a person who is not a member of a couple;
"welfare benefit" means any prescribed benefit, allowance, payment or credit.

(11) Regulations under subsection (10) may not prescribe as welfare benefits–

(a) state pension credit under the State Pension Credit Act 2002, or
(b) retirement pensions under Part 2 or 3 of the Social Security Contributions and Benefits Act 1992.

Commencement (27.11.12 for making regulations; 15.4.13 for all other purposes)

Benefit cap: supplementary

97.–(1) Regulations under section 96 may make different provision for different purposes or cases.

(2) Regulations under section 96 must be made by statutory instrument.

(3) A statutory instrument containing the first regulations under section 96 may not be made unless a draft of the instrument has been laid before, and approved by resolution of, each House of Parliament.

(4) A statutory instrument containing other regulations under section 96 is subject to annulment in pursuance of a resolution of either House of Parliament.

(5) In section 150 of the Social Security Administration Act 1992 (annual up-rating of benefits) after subsection (7) there is inserted–

"(7A) The Secretary of State–

(a) shall in each tax year review the amount specified under subsection (5) of section 96 of the Welfare Reform Act 2012 (benefit cap) to determine whether its relationship with estimated average earnings (within the meaning of that section) has changed, and
(b) after that review may, if the Secretary of State considers it appropriate, include in the draft of an up-rating order provision increasing or decreasing that amount."

(6) *[Omitted]*

Commencement (subs (1)-(4) 27.11.12; subs(5) and (6) 15.4.13)

Benefit offences: disqualifying and sanctionable benefits

117.–(1) In the Social Security Fraud Act 2001, section 6A (meaning of "disqualifying benefit" and "sanctionable benefit") is amended as follows.

(2) In subsection (1), in the definition of "disqualifying benefit", after paragraph (e) there is inserted–

"(f) child tax credit;
(g) working tax credit;

(3) In that subsection, in the definition of "sanctionable benefit", after paragraph (f) there is inserted–

"(fa) child tax credit;
(fb) working tax credit;"

Commencement 1.4.13 and 6.4.13.

Benefit offences: period of sanction

118.–(1) The Social Security Fraud Act 2001 is amended as follows.

(2) Section 6B (loss of benefit in case of conviction, penalty or caution for benefit offence) is amended as follows.

(3) In subsection (11), for "the period of four weeks" there is substituted "the relevant period".

(4) After subsection (11) there is inserted–

"(11A) For the purposes of subsection (11) the relevant period is–
(a) in a case falling within subsection (1)(a) where the benefit offence, or one of them, is a relevant offence, the period of three years,
(b) in a case falling within subsection (1)(a) (but not within paragraph (a) above)), the period of 13 weeks, or
(c) in a case falling within subsection (1)(b) or (c), the period of four weeks."

(5) After subsection (13) there is inserted–

"(14) In this section and section 7 "relevant offence" means–
(a) in England and Wales, the common law offence of conspiracy to defraud, or
(b) a prescribed offence which, in the offender's case, is committed in such circumstances as may be prescribed, and which, on conviction–
 (i) is found by the court to relate to an overpayment (as defined in section 115A(8) of the Administration Act) of at least £50,000,
 (ii) is punished by a custodial sentence of at least one year (including a suspended sentence as defined in section 189(7)(b) of the Criminal Justice Act 2003), or
 (iii) is found by the court to have been committed over a period of at least two years."

(6) After subsection (14) (inserted by subsection (5) above) there is inserted–

"(15) The Secretary of State may by order amend subsection (11A)(a), (b) or (c), or (14)(b)(i), (ii) or (iii) to substitute a different period or amount for that for the time being specified there."

(7) In section 7 (loss of benefit for second or subsequent conviction of benefit offence), after subsection (1) there is inserted–

"(1A) The following restrictions do not apply if the benefit offence referred to in subsection (1)(a), or any of them, is a relevant offence."

(8) In section 11 (loss of benefit regulations)–
(a) in the heading, after "benefit" there is inserted "orders and";
(b) in subsection (3) at the end there is inserted–

"(e) regulations under section 6B(14) or an order under section 6B(15), or";

(c) in subsection (4) after "make", in both places, there is inserted "an order or".

Commencement 1.4.13.

Benefit offences: sanctions for repeated benefit fraud

119.–(1) The Social Security Fraud Act 2001 is amended as follows.

(2) In section 6B (loss of benefit in case of conviction, penalty or caution for benefit offence), in subsection (3) for "later" there is substituted "current".

(3) Section 7 (loss of benefit for second or subsequent conviction of benefit offence) is amended as follows.

(4) In the heading, for "second or subsequent conviction of benefit offence" there is substituted "repeated benefit fraud".

(5) For subsection (1)(a) to (e) there is substituted–

"(a) a person ("the offender") is convicted of one or more benefit offences in a set of proceedings ("the current set of proceedings"),
(b) within the period of five years ending on the date on which the benefit offence was, or any of them were, committed, one or more disqualifying events occurred in relation to the offender (the event, or the most recent of them, being referred to in this section as "the earlier disqualifying event"),
(c) the current set of proceedings has not been taken into account for the purposes of any previous application of this section or section 8 or 9 in relation to the offender or any person who was then a member of his family,
(d) the earlier disqualifying event has not been taken into account as an earlier disqualifying event for the purposes of any previous application of this section or either of those sections in relation to the offender or any person who was then a member of his family, and
(e) the offender is a person with respect to whom the conditions for an entitlement to a sanctionable benefit are or become satisfied at any time within the disqualification period,".

(6) In subsection (6), for the words from "in relation to" to the end, there is substituted "in an offender's case, means the relevant period beginning with a prescribed date falling after the date of the conviction in the current set of proceedings".

(7) After that subsection there is inserted–

"(6A) For the purposes of subsection (6) the relevant period is–
(a) in a case where, within the period of five years ending on the date on which the earlier disqualifying event occurred, a previous disqualifying event occurred in relation to the offender, the period of three years;
(b) in any other case, 26 weeks."

(8) After subsection (7) there is inserted–

"(7A) Subsection (7B) applies where, after the agreement of any person ("P") to pay a penalty under the appropriate penalty provision is taken into account for the purposes of the application of this section in relation to that person–

(a) P's agreement to pay the penalty is withdrawn under subsection (5) of the appropriate penalty provision,

(b) it is decided on an appeal or in accordance with regulations under the Social Security Act 1998 or the Social Security (Northern Ireland) Order 1998 (S.I. 1998/1506 (N.I. 10)) that any overpayment to which the agreement relates is not recoverable or due, or

(c) the amount of any overpayment to which the penalty relates is revised on an appeal or in accordance with regulations under the Social Security Act 1998 or the Social Security (Northern Ireland) Order 1998 and there is no new agreement by P to pay a penalty under the appropriate penalty provision in relation to the revised overpayment.

(7B) In those circumstances, all such payments and other adjustments shall be made as would be necessary if no restriction had been imposed by or under this section that could not have been imposed if P had not agreed to pay the penalty."

(9) In subsection (8), the following definitions are inserted at the appropriate places–

"appropriate penalty provision" has the meaning given in section 6B(2)(a);"
"disqualifying event" has the meaning given in section 6B(13)."

(10) After that subsection there is inserted–

"(8A) Where a person is convicted of more than one benefit offence in the same set of proceedings, there is to be only one disqualifying event in respect of that set of proceedings for the purposes of this section and–

(a) subsection (1)(b) is satisfied if any of the convictions take place in the five year periods mentioned there;

(b) the event is taken into account for the purposes of subsection (1)(d) if any of the convictions have been taken into account as mentioned there;

(c) in the case of the earlier disqualifying event mentioned in subsection (6A)(a), the reference there to the date on which the earlier disqualifying event occurred is a reference to the date on which any of the convictions take place;

(d) in the case of the previous disqualifying event mentioned in subsection (6A)(a), that provision is satisfied if any of the convictions take place in the five year period mentioned there."

(11) After subsection (10) there is inserted–

"(10A) The Secretary of State may by order amend subsection (6A) to substitute different periods for those for the time being specified there.

(10B) An order under subsection (10A) may provide for different periods to apply according to the type of earlier disqualifying event or events occurring in any case".

(12) In section 11 (loss of benefit regulations), in subsection (3), after paragraph (e) (as inserted by section 118 above) there is inserted–

"(f) an order under section 7(10A),".

Commencement 1.4.13

Schedule 2

Section 31

Universal credit: amendments

Social Security Administration Act 1992 (c. 5)

3. The Social Security Administration Act 1992 is amended as follows.

26.–(1) In section 170 (Social Security Advisory Committee), subsection (5) is amended as follows.
(2) In the definition of "the relevant enactments"–

(a) in paragraph (af), for the words from "sections 68" to "to that Act" there is substituted "sections 69 and 70 of the Child Support, Pensions and Social Security Act 2000;";
(b) *[Omitted]*
(3) *[Omitted]*

Social Security Fraud Act 2001 (c. 11)

56. The Social Security Fraud Act 2001 is amended as follows.

57. In section 6A (definitions), in subsection (1), in the definition of "disqualifying benefit", at the beginning there is inserted–

"(za) any benefit under Part 1 of the Welfare Reform Act 2012 (universal credit) or under any provision having ffect in Northern Ireland corresponding to that Part;".

58.–(1) Section 6B (loss of benefit in case of conviction, penalty or caution for benefit offence) is amended as follows.
(2) In subsection (5), for "(6)" there is substituted "(5A)".
(3) *[Omitted]*

59.–(1) Section 7 (loss of benefit for second or subsequent conviction of benefit offence) is amended as follows.
(2) In subsection (2), for "(3)" there is substituted "(2A)".
(3) *[Omitted]*

61.–(1) Section 9 (effect of offence on benefits for members of offender's family) is amended as follows.
(2) In subsection (1), before paragraph (a) there is inserted–

"(za) universal credit;".

(3) In subsection (2), for "or" at the end of paragraph (b) there is substituted "and".
(4) *[Omitted]*

62. In section 10(3) (power to supplement and mitigate loss of benefit provisions) after paragraph (bc) there is inserted–

"(bd) any benefit under Part 1 of the Welfare Reform Act 2012 (universal credit) or under any provision having effect in Northern Ireland corresponding to that Part;".

63.–(1) In section 11 (loss of benefit regulations), subsection (3) is amended as follows.
(3) In paragraph (d) at the end there is inserted "or (aa)".

Commencement 25.2.13

Schedule 3

Section 33

Abolition of benefits: consequential amendments

Social Security Administration Act 1992 (c. 5)

4. The Social Security Administration Act 1992 is amended as follows.

5. In section 7 (relationship between benefits), in subsection (3), for "subsections (1) and (2)" there is substituted "subsection (1)".

Social Security Fraud Act 2001 (c. 11)

15. The Social Security Fraud Act 2001 is amended as follows.

16. In section 6B (loss of benefit for conviction etc), in subsection (5), for "to (10)" there is substituted "and (8)".

17. In section 7 (loss of benefit for repeated conviction etc), in subsection (2), for "to (5)" there is substituted "and (4A)".

18. In section 11 (regulations), in subsection (3)(c), for the words from "section" to the end there is substituted "section 6B(5A) or (8), 7(2A) or (4A) or 9(2A) or (4A)".

Commencement 1.4.13, in so far as the amendments relate to the abolition of council; tax benefit

Schedule 9

Section 91

Personal independence payment: amendments

Social Security Administration Act 1992 (c. 5)

7. The Social Security Administration Act 1992 is amended as follows.

8.–(1) Section 1 (entitlement to benefit dependent on claim) is amended as follows.

(2) In subsection (3)–

(a) before paragraph (a) there is inserted–

"(za) for personal independence payment by virtue of section 82 of the Welfare Reform Act 2012; or";

(b) paragraph (b) and the "or" preceding it is repealed.

(3) In subsection (4), after paragraph (ac) there is inserted–

"(ad) personal independence payment."

9. In section 5(2) (regulations about claims for and payments of benefit), after paragraph (ac) there is inserted–

"(ad) personal independence payment;".

12. In section 121DA (interpretation of Part 6), in subsection (1), after paragraph (hj) (inserted by Schedule 2 to this Act) there is inserted–

"(hk) Part 4 of that Act;".

29. In section 182B (information about postal redirection), in subsection (5)(b), after "Welfare Reform Act 2012" (inserted by Schedule 2 to this Act) there is inserted ', Part 4 of that Act".

31. In section 187 (inalienability), in subsection (1), after paragraph (ac) there is inserted–

"(ad) personal independence payment;".

32. In section 191 (interpretation), in the definition of "benefit", for '', state pension credit and an employment and support allowance" there is substituted "state pension credit, an employment and support allowance and personal independence payment".

45. The Social Security Fraud Act 2001 is amended as follows.

46. In section 6A(1) (definitions)–

(a) in the definition of "disqualifying benefit", after paragraph (c) there is inserted–

"(ca) any benefit under Part 4 of the Welfare Reform Act 2012 (personal independence payment) or under any provision in Northern Ireland which corresponds to that Part;";

(b) in the definition of "sanctionable benefit", after paragraph (c) there is inserted–

"(ca) personal independence payment;".

47. In section 10 (power to supplement and mitigate loss of benefit provisions), in subsection (3), after paragraph (bd) (inserted by Schedule 2 to this Act) there is inserted–

"(be) any benefit under Part 4 of the Welfare Reform Act 2012 (personal independence payment) or under any provision in Northern Ireland which corresponds to that Part;".

Commencement 8.4.13

Schedule 14

Section 147

Repeals

PART 1
ABOLITION OF BENEFITS SUPERSEDED BY UNIVERSAL CREDIT

Short title and chapter	**Extent of repeal**
Social Security Contributions and Benefits Act 1992 (c. 4)	Sections 123 to 137. Section 175(6).
Social Security Administration Act 1992 (c. 5)	Section 6. In section 7– (a) in the heading, the words "community charge benefits and other";

Short title and chapter	Extent of repeal
	(b) subsection (2), so far as not otherwise repealed; (c) subsection (3)(b) and the preceding "and". Sections 110A and 110AA. In section 111– (a) in subsection (1)(ab), "or 110AA"; (b) in subsection (3), "or 110A". In section 115A– (a) in subsection (1), "or an authority", "71A, 75 or 76" and "or authority"; (b) in subsection (1A) (as inserted by section 113 of this Act), "or an authority" in both places and "71A, 75 or 76"; (c) in subsection (2), "or authority", in both places; (d) in subsection (5), "or authority", in both places; (e) subsections (7A) and (7B). In section 115B– (a) in subsection (1), "or an authority that administers housing benefit or council tax benefit"; (b) in subsection (3), "or authority", in both places; (c) in subsection (4)(a) (as substituted by section 102 of this Act), "or authority"; (d) in subsection (4A) (as so substituted), the words from "(and, where" to the end; (e) in subsection (6), "or authority", in both places. In section 116– (a) in subsection (2)(a), "(other than proceedings to which paragraph (b) applies)" (as substituted by section 111 (a) of this Act); (b) subsection (2)(b) and the preceding "and"; (c) subsection (3)(b) and the preceding "and"; (d) subsections (4) and (5). Section 116A. Section 121DA(6). Sections 122C to 122E. Section 128A (and the preceding cross-heading). Sections 138 to 140G. Section 176(1)(a) and (b). Section 182A(3)(c). Section 182B(2). In section 189– (a) subsections (7) and (7A); (b) in subsection (8), "140B, 140C" In section 191, the definitions of– (a) "billing authority"; (d) "council tax benefit scheme"; In Schedule 4, the paragraphs headed "Local authorities etc".
Social Security Administration (Fraud) Act 1997 (c. 47)	Section 3. Section 4(1). Section 5. Sections 8 to 10. In Schedule 1, paragraphs 3 and 7.
Social Security Act 1998 (c. 14)	Section 34. Section 79(8).
Welfare Reform and Pensions Act 1999 (c. 30)	Sections 57 and 58.
Immigration and Asylum Act 1999 (c. 33)	In section 115(1)(k)

Child Support, Pensions and Social Security Act 2000 (c. 19)	Section 68. In Schedule 6, paragraph 3. Schedule 7.
Social Security Fraud Act 2001 (c. 11)	In section 6B– (a) in subsection (2)(b)(i), "or an authority which administers housing benefit or council tax benefit"; (b) subsection (10). In section 7– (a) subsections (3), (4), (4B) and (5); (b) in subsection (10), ''8 or". In section 9– (a) subsection (1)(a), (b), (bc), (c) and (d); (b) subsection (5).
Welfare Reform Act 2007 (c. 5)	Sections 32 to 34
Welfare Reform Act 2012 (c.5)	Section 130(7)(c)

Commencement 1.4.13 in so far as they relate to the abolition of CTB

PART 11
RECOVERY OF BENEFIT PAYMENTS

Short title and chapter	**Extent of repeal**
Social Security Administration Act 1992 (c. 5)	Section 7(2)(a)

Financial Services Act 2012

Further minor and consequential amendments and repeals

114.–(1) Schedule 18 contains further amendments of FSMA 2000 and other enactments.

(2) *[Omitted]*

Schedule 19

Social Security Administration Act 1992 (c. 5)

74.–(1) The Social Security Administration Act 1992 is amended as follows.

(2) *[Omitted]*

(3) In section 109B (power to require information), in subsection (7), in the definitions of "bank" and "insurer", for "Part IV" substitute "Part 4A".

PART III:

REGULATIONS

The Benefit Cap (Housing Benefit) Regulations 2012

(SI 2012 No.2994)

Made	*29th November 2012*
Coming into force	*15th April 2013*

The Secretary of State for Work and Pensions makes the following Regulations in exercise of the powers conferred by sections 96(1), (3), (4)(a), (b), (c) and (g), (5) and (10) and 97(1) of the Welfare Reform Act 2012.

A draft of these Regulations was laid before Parliament in accordance with section 97(3) of the Welfare Reform Act 2012 and approved by a resolution of each House. This instrument contains only regulations made by virtue of, or consequential upon, sections 96 and 97 of the Welfare Reform Act 2012 and is made before the end of the period of six months beginning with the coming into force of those sections.

In accordance with section 176(1) of the Social Security Administration Act 1992, the Secretary of State has consulted with organisations appearing to him to be representative of the authorities concerned.

Citation and commencement

1. These Regulations may be cited as the Benefit Cap (Housing Benefit) Regulations 2012 and come into force on 15th April 2013.

Amendment of the Housing Benefit Regulations 2006

2.–(1) The Housing Benefit Regulations 2006 are amended as follows.

(2) In regulation 2 (interpretation)–

(a) after the definition of "employed earner" insert–

"employment and support allowance" means an employment and support allowance under Part 1 of the Welfare Reform Act;"; and

(b) after the definition of "Jobseekers Act" insert–

"jobseeker's allowance" means a jobseeker's allowance within the meaning of Part 1 of the Jobseekers Act;".

(3) After regulation 72D (relationship between extended payment and entitlement to housing benefit under the general conditions of entitlement) insert–

"**Calculation of an extended payment where the benefit cap applies**

72E. Where a claimant's housing benefit in the benefit week with respect to which the extended payment is to be calculated is reduced in accordance with regulation 75D, the extended payment must be calculated using the amount of housing benefit before any such reduction is made.".

(4) After regulation 73D (relationship between extended payment (qualifying contributory benefits) and entitlement to housing benefit under the general conditions of entitlement) insert–

"**Calculation of an extended payment (qualifying contributory benefits) where the benefit cap applies**

73E. Where a claimant's housing benefit in the benefit week with respect to which the extended payment (qualifying contributory benefits) is to be calculated is reduced in accordance with regulation 75D, the extended payment (qualifying contributory benefits) must be calculated using the amount of housing benefit before any such reduction is made.".

(5) After Part 8 (amount of benefit) insert–

"PART 8A
Benefit cap

Circumstances in which a benefit cap will apply

75A. Unless regulation 75E or 75F applies, a benefit cap applies where the relevant authority makes a determination that during the reference period the total amount of welfare benefits to which–

(a) where the claimant is a member of a couple, each member of the couple is or jointly are entitled; or

(b) in any other case, the claimant is entitled, exceeds the relevant amount.

Determination of whether a benefit cap applies

75B. The relevant authority need not determine whether the benefit cap applies, or whether to change the amount of any reduction made in accordance with regulation 75D, unless it receives notification from the Secretary of State that the benefit cap may apply or that there has been a change in the amount of a welfare benefit to which the claimant is entitled (but nothing shall prevent the relevant authority making a determination as to whether the benefit cap applies, or the amount of any reduction, if it has information or evidence suggesting that it should do so).

Manner of calculating the amount of welfare benefits

75C.–(1) When calculating the total amount of welfare benefits, the relevant authority must use the amount of a welfare benefit to which a person is entitled unless paragraph (2), (3) or (4) applies.

(2) Where the welfare benefit is housing benefit, the relevant authority must not take account of any reduction under regulation 75D and must use the amount to which the claimant would be entitled by virtue of section 130 of the Act.

(3) Where the welfare benefit is an employment and support allowance, the relevant authority must disregard that benefit where a person is disqualified for receiving it by virtue of section 18 of the Welfare Reform Act.

(4) Where an amount of a welfare benefit other than jobseeker's allowance or employment and support allowance is taken into account as income in accordance with Part 6 (income and capital), or would be so taken into account if the relevant authority were required to calculate the claimant's income, the relevant authority must use that amount.

(5) The amount of a welfare benefit for the purpose of paragraph (4) includes any amount of that benefit which would have been payable but for any loss of benefit under, or by virtue of, section 6B, 7 or 9 of the Social Security Fraud Act 2001.

Reduction of housing benefit

75D.–(1) Subject to paragraph (2), where the benefit cap applies, the relevant authority must reduce the amount of housing benefit to which the claimant is entitled by virtue of section 130 of the Act by the amount by which the total amount of welfare benefits exceeds the relevant amount.

(2) Where the reduction would reduce the claimant's housing benefit to less than the minimum amount of housing benefit provided for in regulation 75 (minimum housing benefit) , the relevant authority must reduce the claimant's housing benefit by such amount as will leave the claimant entitled to that minimum amount.

Exception to the benefit cap: current or recent work

75E.–(1) The benefit cap does not apply where paragraph (2) applies or during the period specified in paragraph (3).

(2) This paragraph applies where the claimant is, or the claimant and the claimant's partner are jointly, entitled to working tax credit.

(3) The specified period is, where paragraph (4) applies, the consecutive period of 39 consecutive weeks starting on the day specified in paragraph (5).

(4) This paragraph applies where the relevant authority is satisfied that, for at least 50 weeks out of the 52 weeks immediately preceding their last day of work, the claimant or the claimant's partner ("P")–

(a) was employed or engaged in work for payment, or in the expectation of payment; and

(b) was not entitled to income support, a jobseeker's allowance or an employment and support allowance, and, for the purposes of sub-paragraph (a), P is employed or engaged in work for any day on which P is on maternity leave, paternity leave or adoption leave or is in receipt of statutory sick pay.

(5) The specified day is the day after the last day on which P was employed or engaged in the work referred to in paragraph (4).

Exception to the benefit cap: receipt of specified benefit

75F.–(1) The benefit cap does not apply where–

(a) the claimant or the claimant's partner is receiving an employment and support allowance under Part 1 of the Welfare Reform Act which includes a support component;

(b) the claimant or the claimant's partner is receiving an industrial injuries benefit by virtue of Part 5 of the Act;

(c) the claimant or the claimant's partner is receiving an attendance allowance;

(d) the claimant or the claimant's partner is receiving a war pension;

(e) the claimant, the claimant's partner or a child or young person for whom the claimant or the claimant's partner is responsible, is receiving a disability living allowance;

(f) the claimant, the claimant's partner or a child or young person for whom the claimant or the claimant's partner is responsible is entitled to a payment listed in sub-paragraph (b), (c), (d) or (e) but–

(i) that person is not receiving it under regulation 6 (hospitalisation) or regulation 7 (persons in care homes) of the Social Security (Attendance Allowance) Regulations 1991;

(ii) it is withheld under article 53 of the Naval, Military and Air Forces Etc (Disablement and Death) Service Pensions Order 2006 (maintenance in hospital or an institution);

(iii) that person is not receiving it under regulation 8 (hospitalisation) or regulation 9 (persons in care homes) of the Social Security (Disability Living Allowance) Regulations 1991;

(2) In this regulation "war pension" has the meaning in regulation 2 (interpretation) and includes–

(a) a guaranteed income payment;

(b) a pension payable to a person as a widow, widower or surviving civil partner under any power of Her Majesty otherwise than under an enactment to make provision about pensions for or in respect of persons who have been disabled or have died in consequence of service as members of the armed forces of the Crown;

(c) a payment which is made under any of–

(i) the Order in Council of 19th December 1881;

(ii) the Royal Warrant of 27th October 1884;

(iii) the Order by His Majesty of 14th January 1922,

to a widow, widower or surviving civil partner of a person whose death was attributable to service in a capacity analogous to service as a member of the armed forces of the Crown and whose service in such capacity terminated before 31st March 1973

(d) a pension paid by the government of a country outside Great Britain which is analogous to a war pension or any of the pensions or payments mentioned in subparagraphs (a) to (c).

Interpretation

75G. For the purposes of section 96 of the Welfare Reform Act 2012 and this Part–

"couple" has the meaning in regulation 2 unless the claimant is a member of a polygamous marriage, in which case it means the claimant and the member of the polygamous marriage to whom the claimant was first married and references to the claimant's partner are to that member of that marriage;

"reference period" means a benefit week;

"relevant amount" is–

(a) for a single claimant, £350; and

(b) for all other claimants, £500;

"welfare benefit" means–

(a) bereavement allowance;

(b) carer's allowance;

(c) child benefit;

(d) child tax credit;

(e) an employment and support allowance;

(f) guardian's allowance;

(g) housing benefit;

(h) incapacity benefit;

(i) income support;

(j) a jobseeker's allowance;

(k) maternity allowance;

(l) severe disablement allowance;

(m) widowed mother's allowance ;

(n) widowed parent's allowance;

(o) widow's pension.".

Amendment of the Housing Benefit and Council Tax Benefit (Decisions and Appeals) Regulations 2001

3.–(1) The Housing Benefit and Council Tax Benefit (Decisions and Appeals) Regulations 2001 are amended as follows.

(2) In regulation 4 (revision of decisions) after paragraph (7F) insert–

"(7H) Where a relevant authority has reduced housing benefit as a consequence of regulation 75D of the Housing Benefit Regulations, that decision may be revised at any time.".

(3) In regulation 7(2) (decisions superseding earlier decisions) after sub-paragraph (q) insert–

"(r) which as a consequence of regulation 75D of the Housing Benefit Regulations reduces housing benefit to apply the benefit cap or increases or decreases such a reduction (including a decrease to nil).".

(4) In regulation 8 (date from which a decision superseding an earlier decision takes effect) after paragraph (14E) insert–

"(14F) Where a decision is superseded in accordance with regulation 7(2)(r), the superseding decision shall take effect–

(a) on the date the superseding decision is made where the decision results in the application of the benefit cap or an increase in a reduction; and

(b) where the decision results in the benefit cap ceasing to apply or a decrease in a reduction, on the date from which the welfare benefit (within the meaning of regulation 75G of the Housing Benefit Regulations) is reduced.".

The Housing Benefit (Amendment) Regulations 2012

(SI 2012 No.3040)

Made — *3rd December 2012*
Coming into force in accordance with regulation 1

The Secretary of State for Work and Pensions makes the following Regulations in exercise of the powers conferred by sections 123(1)(d), 130A(2), (3) and (5), 137(1) and 175(1), (3), (4) and (5) of the Social Security Contributions and Benefits Act 1992, section 79(4) of the Social Security Act 1998 and paragraphs 4(4A) and (6), 20(1) and 23(1) of Schedule 7 to the Child Support, Pensions and Social Security Act 2000. A draft of these Regulations was laid before Parliament in accordance with section 176(1)(ab) of the Social Security Contributions and Benefits Act 1992(d) and approved by a resolution of each House.

This instrument contains only regulations made by virtue of, or consequential upon, section 69 of the Welfare Reform Act 2012(e) and is made before the end of the period of six months beginning with the coming into force of that section.

In accordance with section 176(1) of the Social Security Administration Act 1992(f), the Secretary of State has consulted with organisations appearing to him to be representative of the authorities concerned.

Citation, commencement and interpretation

1.–(1) These Regulations may be cited as the Housing Benefit (Amendment) Regulations 2012.

(2) Subject to paragraph (3), these Regulations come into force on 1st January 2013.

(3) Regulations 3(2)(a), 4(2)(a), 5 and 6 come into force on 1st April 2013.

(4) In these Regulations–

"the Housing Benefit Regulations" means the Housing Benefit Regulations 2006; and

"the Housing Benefit (State Pension Credit) Regulations" means the Housing Benefit (Persons who have attained the qualifying age for state pension credit) Regulations 2006.

Amendment of the Housing Benefit and Council Tax Benefit (Decisions and Appeals) Regulations 2001

2.–(1) The Housing Benefit and Council Tax Benefit (Decisions and Appeals) Regulations 2001 are amended as follows.

(2) In regulation 8 (date from which a decision superseding an earlier decision takes effect) for paragraph (15)(c) substitute–

"(15) A decision to which regulation 7A(2) applies shall take effect–

(a) from 1st April in a case where the claimant's weekly amount of eligible rent falls to be calculated in accordance with regulation 80(2)(b) or (c) of the Housing Benefit Regulations or, as the case may be, regulation 61(2)(b) or (c) of the Housing Benefit (State Pension Credit) Regulations; and

(b) in any other case, from the first Monday in April.".

Amendment of the Housing Benefit Regulations relating to the determination of the maximum rent (LHA)

3.–(1) The Housing Benefit Regulations are amended as follows.

(2) In regulation 13C(d) (when a maximum rent (LHA) is to be determined)–

(a) in paragraph (2)(d)–

(i) at the end of paragraph (ii) omit "or"; and

(ii) after paragraph (iii) add–

"or

(iv) notification of a change of a kind which affects the amount of the claimant's cap rent as determined in accordance with regulation 13D (determination of a maximum rent (LHA)).";

(b) for paragraph (3) substitute–

"(3) This paragraph applies on 1st April in any year.";

(c) omit paragraph (4); and
(d) in paragraph (6) omit the definition of "the LHA date".

Amendment of the Housing Benefit (State Pension Credit) Regulations relating to the determination of the maximum rent (LHA)

4.–(1) The Housing Benefit (State Pension Credit) Regulations are amended as follows.

(2) In regulation 13C(e) (when a maximum rent (LHA) is to be determined)–
(a) in paragraph (2)(d)–
(i) at the end of paragraph (ii) omit "or"; a and
(ii) after paragraph (iii) add–

"or
(iv) notification of a change of a kind which affects the amount of the claimant's cap rent as determined in accordance with regulation 13D (determination of a maximum rent (LHA)).";

(b) for paragraph (3) substitute–

"(3) This paragraph applies on 1st April in any year.";

(c) omit paragraph (4); and
(d) in paragraph (6) omit the definition of "the LHA date".

Amendment of the Housing Benefit Regulations relating to the determination of the maximum rent (social sector)

5.–(1) The Housing Benefit Regulations are amended as follows.

(2) In regulation 2(1) (interpretation)–
(a) in the definition of "eligible rent", in paragraph (a) after "regulations 12B (eligible rent)," insert "12BA (eligible rent and maximum rent (social sector)),"; and
(b) in the definition of "registered housing association"–
(i) in paragraph (b) after "Housing Act 1996" add "or a registered social landlord within the meaning of Part 1 of that Act"; and
(ii) in paragraph (c) after "Housing (Scotland) Act 2010" add "or a registered social landlord within the meaning of section 165 of that Act".

(3) In regulation 11(1)(c) (eligible housing costs) after sub-paragraph (a) insert–

"(ab) regulations 12BA (eligible rent and maximum rent (social sector)), A13 (when a maximum rent (social sector) is to be determined) and B13 (determination of a maximum rent (social sector));".

(4) In regulation 12B(d) (eligible rent) for paragraph (1) substitute–

"(1) The amount of a person's eligible rent shall be determined in accordance with the provisions of this regulation except where any of the following provisions applies–
(a) regulation 12BA (eligible rent and maximum rent (social sector));
(b) regulation 12C (eligible rent and maximum rent);
(c) regulation 12D (eligible rent and maximum rent (LHA));
(d) paragraph 4 of Schedule 3 to the Consequential Provisions Regulations.".

(5) After regulation 12B insert–

"Eligible rent and maximum rent (social sector)

12BA.–(1) This regulation applies where a maximum rent (social sector) has been, or is to be, determined in accordance with regulation A13 (when a maximum rent (social sector) is to be determined).

(2) Except where paragraph (3) or (6) applies, the amount of a person's eligible rent is the maximum rent (social sector).

(3) Where the claimant occupies a dwelling which is the same as that occupied by the claimant at the date of death of a linked person, the eligible rent is–

(a) the eligible rent which applied on the day before the death occurred; or

(b) in a case where no eligible rent applied on that day, an eligible rent determined in accordance with regulation 12B(2),

where that eligible rent is more than the eligible rent determined in accordance with paragraph (2).

(4) For the purpose of paragraph (3), a claimant is treated as occupying the dwelling if paragraph (13) of regulation 7 (circumstances in which a person is or is not to be treated as occupying a dwelling as his home) is satisfied and for that purpose paragraph (13) shall have effect as if sub-paragraph (b) of that paragraph were omitted.

(5) Where a person's eligible rent has been determined in accordance with paragraph (3) (protection on death), it shall apply until the first of the following events occurs–

(a) the period of 12 months from the date of death has expired;

(b) the determination of an eligible rent in accordance with paragraph (3) (protection on death) in relation to a subsequent death;

(c) there is a change of circumstances and the relevant authority determines a new eligible rent in accordance with paragraph (2) which is equal to or more than the eligible rent determined in accordance with paragraph (3);

(d) there is a change of dwelling; or

(e) the determination of an eligible rent under regulation 12B.

(6) Where the relevant authority is satisfied that the claimant or a linked person was able to meet the financial commitments for the dwelling when they were entered into, the eligible rent is an eligible rent determined in accordance with regulation 12B(2) where that eligible rent is more than the eligible rent determined in accordance with paragraph (2).

(7) Paragraph (6) shall not apply where the claimant or the claimant's partner was previously entitled to benefit in respect of an award of housing benefit which fell wholly or partly less than 52 weeks before the commencement of the claimant's current award of housing benefit.

(8) Where a person's eligible rent has been determined in accordance with paragraph (6) (13 week protection), it shall apply until the first of the following events occurs–

(a) the first 13 weeks of the claimant's award of housing benefit have expired;

(b) the determination of an eligible rent in accordance with paragraph (3) (protection on death);

(c) there is a change of circumstances and the relevant authority determines a new eligible rent in accordance with paragraph (2) which is equal to or more than the eligible rent determined in accordance with paragraph (6);

(d) there is a change of dwelling; or

(e) the determination of an eligible rent under regulation 12B.".

(6) In regulation 12D(a) (eligible rent and maximum rent (LHA)), in paragraph (7)(a)(iv) and (b)(iv) after "regulation 13" insert ", a maximum rent (social sector) by virtue of regulation A13".

(7) After regulation 12M(b) (transitional protection – reduction in LHA) insert–

"When a maximum rent (social sector) is to be determined

A13.–(1) Subject to paragraph (2), the relevant authority must determine a maximum rent (social sector) in accordance with regulation B13 (determination of a maximum rent (social sector)) where the relevant authority has not determined, and is not required to determine–

(a) a maximum rent in accordance with regulation 13 (maximum rent); or
(b) a maximum rent (LHA) by virtue of regulation 13C (when a maximum rent (LHA) is to be determined).
(2) This regulation does not apply–
(a) in a rent allowance case where the tenancy is an excluded tenancy of a type mentioned in any of paragraphs 4 to 11 of Schedule 2 (excluded tenancies) and the landlord is not a registered housing association;
(b) in respect of shared ownership tenancies;
(c) in respect of mooring charges for houseboats and payments in respect of the site on which a caravan or mobile home stands;
(d) where the claimant or the claimant's partner has attained the qualifying age for state pension credit, or where both have attained that age; or
(e) where the dwelling is temporary accommodation.
(3) In this regulation "temporary accommodation" means accommodation of a kind listed in paragraph (4) which the relevant authority makes available to the claimant, or which a registered housing association makes available to the claimant in pursuance of arrangements made with it by the authority–
(a) to discharge any of the authority's functions under Part 3 of the Housing Act 1985, Part 7 of the Housing Act 1996 or (in Scotland) Part 2 of the Housing (Scotland) Act 1987; or
(b) to prevent the claimant being or becoming homeless within the meaning of Part 7 of the Housing Act 1996 or (in Scotland) Part 2 of the Housing (Scotland) Act 1987.
(4) The accommodation referred to in paragraph (3) is–
(a) accommodation–
(i) provided for a charge, where that charge includes the provision of that accommodation and some cooked or prepared meals which are also cooked or prepared, and consumed, in that accommodation or associated premises; or
(ii) provided in a hotel, guest house, lodging house or similar establishment, but does not include accommodation which is provided in a care home, an independent hospital or a hostel;
(b) accommodation which the authority or registered housing association holds on a lease and, in the case of an authority in England, is held outside the Housing Revenue Account on a lease granted for a term not exceeding 10 years;
(c) accommodation which the authority or registered housing association has a right to use under an agreement other than a lease with a third party.

Determination of a maximum rent (social sector)

B13.–(1) The maximum rent (social sector) is determined in accordance with paragraphs (2) to (4).
(2) The relevant authority must determine a limited rent by–
(a) determining the amount that the claimant's eligible rent would be in accordance with regulation 12B(2) without applying regulation 12B(4) and (6);
(b) where the number of bedrooms in the dwelling exceeds the number of bedrooms to which the claimant is entitled in accordance with paragraph (5), reducing that amount by the appropriate percentage set out in paragraph (3); and
(c) where more than one person is liable to make payments in respect of the dwelling, apportioning the amount determined in accordance with sub-paragraphs (a) and (b) between each such person having regard to all the circumstances, in particular, the number of such persons and the proportion of rent paid by each person.
(3) The appropriate percentage is–
(a) 14% where the number of bedrooms in the dwelling exceeds by one the number of bedrooms to which the claimant is entitled; and
(b) 25% where the number of bedrooms in the dwelling exceeds by two or more the number of bedrooms to which the claimant is entitled.

(4) Where it appears to the relevant authority that in the particular circumstances of any case the limited rent is greater than it is reasonable to meet by way of housing benefit, the maximum rent (social sector) shall be such lesser sum as appears to that authority to be an appropriate rent in that particular case.

(5) The claimant is entitled to one bedroom for each of the following categories of person whom the relevant authority is satisfied occupies the claimant's dwelling as their home (and each person shall come within the first category only which is applicable)–

(a) a couple (within the meaning of Part 7 of the Act);
(b) a person who is not a child;
(c) two children of the same sex;
(d) two children who are less than 10 years old;
(e) a child,

and one additional bedroom in any case where the claimant or the claimant's partner is a person who requires overnight care (or in any case where each of them is).".

(8) In Schedule 2 (excluded tenancies) in paragraph 3–
(a) omit sub-paragraph (2)(a); and
(b) in sub-paragraph (3) omit "(a) or".

(9) In Part 2 (application of the regulations) of Schedule 10 (former pathfinder authorities) for paragraph 4 substitute–

"4. In regulation 12B(1) (eligible rent) after sub-paragraph (c) insert–
"(ca) any of regulations 12E to 12K (transitional protection for pathfinder cases);".".

Amendment of the Housing Benefit (State Pension Credit) Regulations

6.–(1) The Housing Benefit (State Pension Credit) Regulations are amended as follows.

(2) In regulation 2(1) (interpretation) in the definition of "registered housing association"–

(a) in paragraph (b) after "Housing Act 1996" add "or a registered social landlord within the meaning of Part 1 of that Act"; and
(b) in paragraph (c) after "Housing (Scotland) Act 2010" add "or a registered social landlord within the meaning of section 165 of that Act".

The Welfare Reform Act 2012 (Commencement No.8 and Savings and Transitional Provisions) Order 2013

(SI 2013 No.358)

Made *19th February 2013*

The Secretary of State for Work and Pensions makes the following Order in exercise of the powers conferred by section 150(3) and (4)(a), (b)(iii) and (c) of the Welfare Reform Act 2012.

Citation and interpretation

1.–(1) This Order may be cited as the Welfare Reform Act 2012 (Commencement No.8 and Savings and Transitional Provisions) Order 2013.

(2) In this Order–

"the 1992 Act" means the Social Security Administration Act 1992;

"the 2012 Act" means the Welfare Reform Act 2012;

"personal independence payment" means a payment under Part 4 of the 2012 Act.

Appointed day for council tax benefit

8. 1st April 2013 is the day appointed for the coming into force of the following provisions of the 2012 Act–

(a) section 33(1)(e) (abolition of benefits – council tax benefit);

(b) paragraphs 5 (and paragraph 4 in so far as it relates to paragraph 5) and 15 to 18 of Schedule 3 (abolition of benefits: consequential amendments), and section 33(3) in so far as it relates to those paragraphs, in so far as they relate to the abolition of council tax benefit; and

(c) the provisions of Part 1 of Schedule 14 (repeals – abolition of benefits superseded by universal credit) which are specified in Schedule 4 to this Order in so far as they relate to the abolition of council tax benefit.

Savings for council tax benefit

9. Notwithstanding the coming into force of Part 1 of Schedule 14 to the 2012 Act under article 8(c), the provisions specified in Schedule 4 to this Order and any regulations or orders made under them continue to have effect for any of the following matters arising on or after 1st April 2013 that relate to council tax benefit before 1st April 2013–

(a) the administration of council tax benefit;

(b) the administration of appeals against council tax benefit decisions;

(c) the investigation and prosecution of offences relating to council tax benefit;

(d) the recovery of excess council tax benefit;

(e) the administration of civil and administrative penalties;

(f) the payment of subsidy in respect of council tax benefit for years up to and including the year ending 31st March 2013.

Transitional provisions for council tax benefit

10.–(1) For the purpose of allowing a billing authority, or in Scotland a local authority, to make decisions in relation to matters in respect of council tax benefit arising before 1st April 2013 where a claim is received on or after 1st April 2013–

(a) the Council Tax Benefit Regulations 2006 as saved by virtue of article 9 are modified in accordance with Part 1 of Schedule 5 to this Order; and

(b) the Council Tax Benefit (Persons who have attained the qualifying age for state pension credit) Regulations 2006 as saved by virtue of article 9 are modified in accordance with Part 2 of Schedule 5 to this Order.

(2) In this article–

"billing authority" has the meaning given in Part 1 of the Local Government Finance Act 1992; and "local authority" means a council constituted under section 2 of the Local Government etc.

SCHEDULE 4

Article 8(c)

Commencement of Repeals

Short title and chapter	Extent of repeal
Social Security Contributions and Benefits Act 1992 (c. 4)	Sections 123 to 137. Section 175(6).
Social Security Administration Act 1992 (c. 5)	Section 6. In section 7– (a) in the heading, the words "community charge benefits and others"; (b) subsection (2), so far as not otherwise repealed; (c) subsection (3)(b) and the preceding "and". Sections 110A to 110AA. In section 111– (a) in subsection (1)(ab), "or 110AA"; (b) in subsection (3), "or 110A". In section 115A– (a) in subsection (1), "or an authority", ''1A, 75 or 76" and "or authority"; (b) in subsection (1A) (as inserted by section 113 of the 2012 Act), "or an authority" in both places and ''71A, 75 or 76"; (c) in subsection (2), "or authority", in both places; (d) in subsection (5), "or authority", in both places; (e) subsections (7A) and (7B). In section 115B– (a) in subsection (1), "or an authority that administers housing benefit or council tax benefit"; (b) in subsection (3), "or authority", in both places; (c) in subsection (4)(a) (as substituted by section 102 of the 2012 Act), "or authority"; (d) in subsection (4A) (as so substituted), the words from "(and, where" to the end; (e) in subsection (6), "or authority", in both places. In section 116– (a) in subsection (2)(a), "(other than proceedings to which paragraph (b) applies)" (as substituted by section 111 (a) of the 2012 Act); (b) subsection (2)(b) and the preceding "and"; (c) subsection (3)(b) and the preceding "and"; (d) subsections (4) and (5). Section 116A. Section 121DA(6). Sections 122C to 122E. Section 128A (and the preceding crossheading). Sections 138 to 140G. Section 176(1)(a) and (b). Section 182A(3)(c). Section 182B(2).In section 189– (a) subsections (7) and (7A); (b) in subsection (8), "140B, 140C". In section 191, the definitions of– (a) "billing authority"; (b) "council tax benefit scheme". In Schedule 4, the paragraphs headed "Local authorities etc".
Local Government Finance Act 1992 (c. 14)	In Schedule 9, paragraphs 1 to 13, 15 to 17, 19 to 24 and 25(a) and (c).
Jobseekers Act 1995 (c. 18)	Section 28.

Short title and chapter	Extent of repeal
Social Security Administration (Fraud) Act 1997 (c. 47)	Section 3. Section 4(1). Section 5. Sections 8 to 10. In Schedule 1, paragraphs 3 and 7.
Social Security Act 1998 (c. 14)	Section 34. Section 79(8).
Audit Commission Act 1998 (c. 18)	Sections 38 and 39. Section 50. In Schedule 1, paragraph 8(2)(b).
Scotland Act 1998 (c. 46)	In Part 2 of Schedule 5, in Section F1, under the heading "Illustrations", "administration and funding of housing benefit and council tax benefit;".
Local Government Act 1999 (c. 27)	Section 13A(4A). Section 29(2A).
Welfare Reform and Pensions Act 1999 (c. 30)	Sections 57 and 58.
Immigration and Asylum Act 1999 (c. 33)	Section 115(1)(e), (j) and (k).
Child Support, Pensions and Social Security Act 2000 (c. 19)	Section 68. In Schedule 6, paragraph 3.Schedule 7.
Social Security Fraud Act 2001 (c. 11)	Section 1(5). Section 2(2). Section 6. In section 6B– (a) in subsection (2)(b)(i), "or an authority which administers housing benefit or council tax benefit"; (b) subsections (6), (7), (9) and (10). In section 7– (a) subsections (3), (4), (4B) and (5); (b) in subsection (10), ''8 or". In section 9– (a) subsection (1)(a), (b), (bc), (c) and (d); (b) subsections (3), (4), (4B) and (5). Section 14.
Public Audit (Wales) Act 2004 (c. 23)	In Schedule 2, paragraph 15.
Pensions Act 2004 (c. 35)	In Schedule 10, paragraph 3.
Welfare Reform Act 2007 (c. 5)	Sections 30 to 34. Sections 37 to 39. Section 41(2)(a) to (d) and (3). Sections 46 and 47. Section 48(1) to (3). In Schedule 5, paragraphs 1, 3 to 9, 12 and 13.
Local Government and Public Involvement in Health Act 2007 (c. 50)	Section 147(2). Section 148(1)(b). Section 150.
Welfare Reform Act 2009 (c. 24)	Sections 35 and 36.
Welfare Reform Act 2012 (c. 5)	Section 130(7)(b) and (c).

SCHEDULE 5

Article 10(1)

Modifications

PART 1

Modification of the Council Tax Benefit Regulations 2006

1. The Council Tax Benefit Regulations 2006 are modified as follows.

2. In regulation 69 (time and manner in which claims are to be made)–

(a) in paragraph (1), for "paragraphs (4A) to (4AE)" substitute "paragraph (4A)";

(b) omit paragraph (3);

(c) in paragraph (4)–

(i) omit sub-paragraphs (a), (c) and (f); and

(ii) in sub-paragraph (b) omit "where it has not been sent or delivered to the appropriate DWP office,";

(d) omit paragraphs (4AA) to (4AE);

(e) omit paragraph (4BA);

(f) in paragraph (4C)–
(i) for "paragraphs (4A) to (4AE)" substitute "paragraph (4A)"; and
(ii) omit "or the Secretary of State";
(g) in paragraphs (4E) and (4F) omit "or the Secretary of State";
(h) in paragraph (5)–
(i) in sub-paragraph (b) omit "or appropriate DWP office";
(ii) in sub-paragraph (d), for ", an authorised office, county offices or an appropriate DWP office" substitute "or county offices";
(iii) in sub-paragraph (d) in paragraphs (i) and (ii) omit ", an authorised office or an appropriate DWP office";
(iv) in sub-paragraph (d)(ii), for "paragraphs (4A) to (4AE)" substitute "paragraph (4A)"; and
(v) in sub-paragraph (e), for "authorised office, county offices or appropriate DWP office" substitute "or county offices";
(i) in paragraph (6) omit "or appropriate DWP office";
(j) omit paragraph (7A);
(k) in paragraph (8), for ", (b) or (c)" substitute "or (b)";
(l) in paragraph (8A)–
(i) at the end of sub-paragraph (b) omit "or"; and
(ii) omit sub-paragraph (c); and
(m) omit paragraph (15).
3. In regulation 72 (evidence and information)–
(a) in paragraph (1)–
(i) for "paragraphs (1A) and (2)" substitute "paragraph (2)"; and
(ii) omit ", or the Secretary of State requesting him,"; and
(b) omit paragraph (1A).
4. In regulation 73 (amendment and withdrawal of claim)–
(a) in paragraph (2), for "paragraphs (4A) to (4AE)" substitute "paragraph (4A)";
(b) omit paragraph (5); and
(c) in paragraph (6) omit "or (5)".
5. In regulation 74 (duty to notify changes of circumstances)–
(a) in paragraph (1), for "paragraphs (3), (5) and (7)" substitute "paragraphs (3) and (5)"; and
(b) omit paragraph (7).

PART 2

Modification of the Council Tax Benefit (Persons who have attained the qualifying age for state pension credit) Regulations 2006

1. The Council Tax Benefit (Persons who have attained the qualifying age for state pension credit) Regulations 2006 are modified as follows.

2. In regulation 53 (time and manner in which claims are to be made)–
(a) in paragraph (1), for "paragraphs (4A) to (4BD)" substitute "paragraph (4A)";
(b) omit paragraph (3);
(c) in paragraph (4)–
(i) omit sub-paragraphs (a), (c) and (f); and
(ii) in sub-paragraph (b) omit "where it has not been sent or delivered to the appropriate DWP office,";
(d) omit paragraphs (4B) to (4BD);
(e) omit paragraph (4CA);
(f) in paragraph (4D)–
(i) for "paragraphs (4A) to (4BD)" substitute "paragraph (4A)"; and
(ii) omit "or the Secretary of State";
(g) omit paragraph (4EA);
(h) in paragraphs (4F) and (4G) omit "or the Secretary of State";
(i) in paragraph (5)–
(i) in sub-paragraph (b) omit "or appropriate social security office";
(ii) in sub-paragraph (d), for ", an authorised office, county offices or an appropriate DWP office" substitute "or county offices";
(iii) in sub-paragraph (d) in paragraphs (i) and (ii) omit ", an authorised office or an appropriate DWP office";
(iv) in sub-paragraph (d)(ii), for "paragraphs (4A) to (4BD)" substitute "paragraph (4A)"; and
(v) in sub-paragraph (e), for "or authorised office, county offices or appropriate DWP office" substitute "or county offices";
(j) in paragraph (6) omit "or appropriate DWP office";
(k) omit paragraph (7A);
(l) in paragraph (8), for ", (b) or (c)" substitute "or (b)";

(m) in paragraph (8A)–
   (i) at the end of sub-paragraph (b) omit "or"; and
   (ii) omit sub-paragraph (c); and
(n) omit paragraph (14).

3. In regulation 57 (evidence and information)–
(a) in paragraph (1)–
   (i) for "paragraphs (1A) and (2)" substitute "paragraph (2)"; and
   (ii) omit ", or the Secretary of State requesting him,"; and
(b) omit paragraph (1A).

4. In regulation 58 (amendment and withdrawal of claim)–
(a) in paragraph (2), for "paragraphs (4A) to (4BD)" substitute "paragraph (4A)";
(b) omit paragraph (5); and
(c) in paragraph (6) omit "or (5)".

5. In regulation 59 (duty to notify changes of circumstances)–
(a) in paragraph (1), for "paragraphs (3), (5) to (8) and (10)" substitute "paragraphs (3) and (5) to (8)"; and
(b) omit paragraph (10).

The Social Security (Overpayments and Recovery) Regulations 2013

(SI 2013 No.384)

Made	*25th February2013*
Laid before Parliament	*4th March 2013*
Coming into force in accordance with regulations 1(2) and(3)	

The Secretary of State for Work and Pensions makes the following Regulations in exercise of the powers conferred by sections 71(4), (6)(a) and (b), (8) and (9A) to (9C), 71ZA, 71ZB(2)(b) to (5), 71ZC(1) to (3), 71ZD, 71ZF 71ZG(5), 71ZH(5), 74(2), 75(4), (5)(a) and (8) to (10), 78(2) and 3

(3C) to (3E), 115B(4A), 115C(5), 115D(5), 189(1), (4) to (6) and 191 of the Social Security

Administration Act 1992 ("the Act") and paragraphs 1(1) and 6(b) of Schedule 6 to the Welfare

Reform Act 2012.

In accordance with section 173(1)(b) of the Act, the Secretary of State has obtained the agreement of the Social Security Advisory Committee that proposals in respect of these Regulations should not be referred to it.

In relation to provisions in these Regulations relating to housing benefit, in accordance with section 176(1) of the Act, consultation has taken place with organisations appearing to the Secretary of State to be representative of the authorities concerned.

Citation and commencement

1.–(1) These Regulations may be cited as the Social Security (Overpayments and Recovery) Regulations 2013.

(2) The following provisions of these Regulations come into force on 8th April 2013–

(a) this Part;
(b) Part 6 and Schedules 1 and 2;
(c) [Omitted]
(d) regulation 33(1), (2)(a) and (c) and (3); and
(e) regulation 34(1), (2)(a) and (c) and (3).

(3) All other provisions of these Regulations come into force on 29th April 2013.

Interpretation

2. In these Regulations–

"the Act" means the Social Security Administration Act 1992;
"liable person" means the person from whom a recoverable amount is recoverable;
"recoverable amount" is to be construed in accordance with regulation 3;

PART 2
Recoverability

Recoverable amounts

3.–(1) In these Regulations, "recoverable amount" means–

(a) subject to regulations 7 to 9, the amount of any overpayment; and
(b) any other amount recoverable under any provision of the Act specified in paragraph (2).

(2) Those provisions are–

(a)-(c) *[Omitted]*
(d) section 115B(4)(recovery of penalties imposed as an alternative to prosecution);
(e) section 115C(4) (recovery of civil penalties for incorrect statements); and
(f) section 115D(4) (recovery of civil penalties for failure to disclose information).

PART 6
Recovery by deduction from earnings

Interpretation of Part 6

17.–(1) In this Part–

"appropriate authority", in relation to any recoverable amount, means–

(a) the Secretary of State; or

(b) an authority administering housing benefit if the recoverable amount is recoverable by that authority under section 115B(4)(a), 115C or 115D of the Act,

and where a notice has been issued, "the appropriate authority" means the appropriate authority which issued the notice;

"notice" means a notice issued by an appropriate authority requiring an employer to make deductions from earnings to be paid by the employer to a liable person employed by them and to pay corresponding amounts to that appropriate authority in respect of the recovery of a recoverable amount from the liable person;

"pay-day" in relation to a liable person means an occasion on which earnings are paid to them or the day on which such earnings would normally fall to be paid;

"protected earnings proportion", in relation to a deduction by an employer from a liable person's net earnings, is 60 per cent. of the liable person's net earnings during the period to which the deduction relates, as calculated by the liable person's employer on the relevant payday.

(2) In this Part, subject to paragraph (3), "earnings" means any sums payable to a person–

(a) by way of wages or salary (including any fees, bonus, commission, overtime pay or other emoluments payable in addition to wages or salary payable under a contract of service);

(b) by way of pension which is paid with wages or salary (including an annuity in respect of past service, whether or not rendered to the person paying the annuity, and including periodical payments by way of compensation for the loss, abolition or relinquishment, or diminution in the emoluments, of any office or employment); or

(c) by way of statutory sick pay.

(3) "Earnings" does not include–

(a) sums payable by any public department of the Government of Northern Ireland or of a territory outside the United Kingdom;

(b) pay or allowances payable to the liable person as a member of Her Majesty's forces other than pay or allowances payable by their employer to them as a special member of a reserve force (within the meaning of the Reserve Forces Act 1996);

(c) other pensions, allowances or benefit payable under any enactment relating to social security;

(d) pension or allowances payable in respect of disablement or disability;

(e) guaranteed minimum pension within the meaning of the Pension Schemes Act 1993;

(f) working tax credit payable under section 10 of the Tax Credits Act 2002;

(g) sums paid to reimburse expenses wholly and necessarily incurred in the course of the employment.

(4) "Net earnings" means the residue of earnings after deduction of–

(a) income tax;

(b) primary Class I contributions under Part 1 of the Social Security Contributions and Benefits Act 1992;

(c) amounts deductible by way of contributions to a superannuation scheme which provides for the payment of annuities or lump sums–

(i) to the employee on retirement at a specified age or on becoming incapacitated at some earlier age; or

(ii) on the employee's death or otherwise, to their personal representative, widow, surviving civil partner, relatives or dependants.

(5) Where these Regulations refer to a notice or notification being given or sent, if sent by post to the last known address of the recipient, it is to be treated as having been given or sent on the day on which it is posted.

Exemption from this Part

18. This Part does not impose any obligation on an employer who is carrying on a business which is–

(a) a new business; or

(b) an existing micro-business during the exemption period,

and Schedule 1 has effect for the purpose of this regulation.

Notices

19.–(1) A notice must be given or sent to–

(a) the liable person; and

(b) any employer of the liable person who is to make deductions from the liable person's earnings in accordance with the notice.

(2) A notice must specify–

(a) the full name and address of the liable person;

(b) the name of the employer at whom the notice is directed;

(c) where known, the liable person's place of work, the nature of their work and any staff number, pay roll number or similar identifying number;

(d) the liable person's national insurance number;

(e) the rate at which deductions are be made in accordance with regulation 20(3)(a) or as the case may be, (b) or, if applicable, the deduction to be made in accordance with regulation 20(3)(c);

(f) the protected earnings proportion;

(g) the address to which amounts deducted from earnings are to be sent if paid by cheque; and

(h) details of the account into which such amounts are to be transferred if paid by direct credit transfer.

(3) The notice has effect from the next pay-day which falls a minimum of 22 days after the day on which it is given or sent.

(4) References in paragraphs (1) to (3) to a notice include references to a notice as varied in accordance with regulation 25(1).

Amount to be deducted by employer

20.–(1) This regulation applies where an employer has received from an appropriate authority a notice in respect of a liable person in their employment.

(2) Subject to the following provisions of this regulation, the employer must, each pay-day, make a deduction in accordance with paragraph (3) from the net earnings which it would otherwise pay to the liable person on that pay-day.

(3) The amount to be deducted is–

(a) where the liable person's earnings are payable weekly, the percentage of their earnings specified in column 2 of Table A in Schedule 2 opposite the band in column 1 of that Table within which their net earnings payable on their pay-day fall;

(b) where the liable person's earnings are payable monthly, the percentage of their earnings specified in column 2 of Table B in that Schedule opposite the band in column 1 of that Table within which their net earnings payable on their pay-day fall; or

(c) a lower amount calculated in the manner specified by the appropriate authority in the notice.

(4) Where any amount calculated under paragraph (3) includes a fraction of a penny, it is to be rounded to the nearest whole penny with a result of exactly half a penny being rounded down to the nearest whole penny below.

(5) The employer must continue to make deductions in accordance with paragraph (3) unless and until they are notified by the appropriate authority that the notice–

(a) has been varied in accordance with regulation 25;

(b) has been discharged under regulation 26; or

(c) has lapsed under regulation 27.

(6) Where, on any pay-day ("the relevant pay-day"), the employer fails to deduct an amount under paragraph (3) or deducts an amount less than the amount specified in that paragraph, the employer must, on the next available pay-day or pay-days, first deduct the amount required to be deducted under paragraph (3) for that pay-day and then the difference between the amount, if any, which was deducted on the relevant pay-day and the amount which should have been deducted on that pay-day.

(7) Where a deduction made in accordance with paragraph (3) or (6) would reduce the amount paid to the liable person below the protected earnings proportion, the employer must deduct only such amount as will result in the employer paying the liable person an amount equal to the protected earnings proportion.

(8) Where, on any pay-day ("the relevant pay-day"), the employer deducts more than the amount required to be deducted under paragraph (3), the employer must, on the next available pay-day or pay-days, deduct only the amount required to be deducted under paragraph (3) less the difference between the amount which was deducted on the relevant pay-day and the amount which should have been deducted on that pay-day.

(9) Where, on any pay-day, an employer makes a deduction from the earnings of a liable person in accordance with the notice, they may also deduct an additional amount not exceeding £1 in respect of their administrative costs and such deduction for administrative costs may reduce the amount which the employer pays to the liable person on that pay-day below the protected earnings proportion.

Employer to notify liable person of deduction

21.–(1) An employer making a deduction from earnings for the purposes of these Regulations must notify the liable person in writing of–

(a) the amount of the deduction including any amount deducted for administrative costs under regulation 20(9); and

(b) how that amount was calculated.

(2) Such notification must be given or sent not later than the pay-day on which the deduction is made or, where that is impracticable, not later than the following pay-day.

Payment by employer to the appropriate authority

22.–(1) Amounts deducted by an employer pursuant to regulation 20 (other than any administrative costs deducted under paragraph (9) of that regulation) must be paid by the employer to the appropriate authority by the 19th day of the month following the month in which the deduction is made.

(2) Such payment may be made–

(a) by cheque;

(b) by direct credit transfer; or

(c) by such other method as the appropriate authority may permit.

(3) The employer must keep a record of every amount paid to an appropriate authority pursuant to paragraph (1) and of the employee in respect of whom each such amount was paid.

Information to be provided by the liable person

23.–(1) A liable person who has been given or sent a notice in accordance with regulation 19(1)(a) must notify the appropriate authority in writing within 7 days of each occasion on which–

(a) they leave the employment of an employer named in a notice issued by the appropriate authority in respect of them; or

(b) they become employed or re-employed.

(2) A notification under paragraph (1)(b) must include the following details–

(a) the name and address of their employer or employers if more than one;

(b) the amount of their earnings or expected earnings; and
(c) their place of work, nature of their work and any staff number, pay roll number or similar identifying number.

Duty of employers and others to notify appropriate authority

24.–(1) In this regulation, "P" means the liable person.

(2) Where a notice is given or sent to a person who is believed to be an employer of P but P is not in that person's employment, that person must notify the appropriate authority of that fact in writing, at the address specified in the notice, within 10 days after the day on which the notice is given or sent.

(3) In paragraphs (4) and (5), "E" means an employer of P.

(4) Where a notice is given or sent to E but E believes that there is no obligation on them under this Part by virtue of regulation 18 and Schedule 1, E must notify the appropriate authority of that fact in writing, at the address specified in the notice, within 10 days after the day on which the notice is given or sent.

(5) Where E is required to make deductions under a notice and P ceases to be in their employment, E must notify the appropriate authority of that fact in writing, at the address specified in the notice, within 10 days after the day on which P ceased to be in their employment.

Power to vary notices

25.–(1) The appropriate authority may vary a notice so as to–
(a) decrease any amount to be deducted under regulation 20; or
(b) with the agreement of the liable person, increase any such amount but only to the extent that such deductions will result in the employer paying the liable person an amount more than, or equal to, the protected earnings proportion.

(2) Where a notice has been varied and a copy of the notice as varied has been given or sent in accordance with regulation 19(1) and (4), any employer who is liable to make deductions under the notice must comply with the notice as varied from the day it takes effect by virtue of regulation 19(3).

Discharge of notices

26.–(1) The appropriate authority must discharge a notice where the recoverable amount is no longer outstanding.

(2) The appropriate authority may discharge a notice where–
(a) it appears to them to be defective;
(b) it appears to them that it is ineffective or that some other method of recovering the recoverable amount would be more effective; or
(c) the liable person agrees with the appropriate authority to pay the recoverable amount by another method.

(3) A notice may be considered to be defective for the purpose of paragraph (2)(a) where it does not comply with the requirements of regulation 19(2) and such failure to comply has made it impracticable for an employer to comply with their obligations under these Regulations.

(4) Notification of the discharge of the notice under paragraph (1) or (2) must be given or sent to the liable person and the employer from whom deductions from the liable person's earnings were being made.

(5) Where a notice is discharged by virtue of paragraph (2)(b) or (c), regulation 22 nevertheless applies in respect of any deductions made in respect of the employment but not yet paid to the appropriate authority.

Lapse of notices

27.–(1) Where a liable person in respect of whom deductions are being made in accordance with a notice ceases to be in the employment of an employer, subject to paragraph (2), the notice is to lapse immediately after the pay-day coinciding with, or, if none, the pay-day following, the termination of the employment.

(2) Where a notice lapses by virtue of paragraph (1), regulation 22 nevertheless applies in respect of any deductions made or to be made in respect of the employment but not yet paid to the appropriate authority.

Crown employment

28. There a liable person is in the employment of the Crown and a notice is to be sent in respect of that person, then for the purposes of these Regulations–

(a) the chief officer for the time being of the Department, office or other body in which the liable person is employed is to be treated as having the liable person in their employment (any transfer of the liable person from one Department, office or body to another being treated as a change of employment); and

(b) any earnings paid by the Crown or a minister of the Crown, or out of the public revenue of the United Kingdom, is to be treated as paid by that chief officer.

Priority as between notices and orders requiring deduction from earnings

29.–(1) In this regulation–

"child support order" means a deduction from earnings order under Part 3 of the Child Support (Collection and Enforcement) Regulations 1992;

"other deduction order" means an order, other than a child support order, under any other enactment relating to England and Wales which requires deduction from a person's earnings.

(2) Paragraphs (3) to (10) have effect subject to paragraph (11).

(3) Paragraph (4) applies where an employer would otherwise be obliged, on any pay-day, to make deductions from the earnings which it would otherwise pay to the liable person on that payday under two or more notices.

(4) Where this paragraph applies, the employer must make deductions under the notices according to the respective dates on which they were made, disregarding any later notice until deductions have been made under the earlier one.

(5) Paragraph (6) applies where an employer would otherwise be obliged, on any pay-day, to make deductions from the earnings which it would otherwise pay to the liable person on that payday, under one or more notices and one or more child support orders.

(6) Where this paragraph applies, the employer must first make deductions under the child support order or orders and then make deductions under the notice or notices.

(7) In England and Wales, paragraph (8) applies where an employer would otherwise be obliged, on any pay-day, to make deductions from the earnings which it would otherwise pay to the liable person on that pay-day, under one or more notices and one or more other deduction orders.

(8) Where this paragraph applies, the employer must–

(a) in a case where there is at least one other deduction order in effect on the first pay-day in respect of which deductions would otherwise be made under the notice, first make deductions under the other deduction order or orders and then under any notice or notices;

(b) in any other case, make deductions under the other deduction order and the notices according to the respective dates on which they were made, disregarding any later notice or order until deductions have been made under the earlier one.

(9) In Scotland, paragraph (10) applies where an employer would otherwise be obliged, on any pay-day, to make deductions from the earnings which it would otherwise pay to the liable person on that pay-day, under one or more notices and one or more diligences against earnings.

(10) Where this paragraph applies, the employer must–

(a) in a case where there is a diligence against earnings in effect on the first pay-day in respect of which deductions would otherwise be made under the notice, first make deductions under any diligence against earnings and then under any notice;

(b) in any other case, make deductions under any notice and then under any diligence against earnings.

(11) An employer may only make deductions under paragraph (4), (6), (8) or (10) up to the extent that such deductions will result in the employer paying the liable person an amount equal to or greater than the protected earnings proportion.

Offences

30. A person who fails to comply with any of the following provisions of this Part is guilty of an offence punishable on summary conviction by a fine not exceeding level 3 on the standard scale–

(a) regulation 20(2);
(b) regulation 22(1);
(c) regulation 22(3);
(d) regulation 23.

PART 8

Amendment of provisions relating to recovery of overpaid housing benefit

Amendment of the Housing Benefit Regulations 2006

33.–(1) The Housing Benefit Regulations 2006 are amended as follows.

(2) In regulation 105 (recovery of overpayments from prescribed benefits–

(a) after paragraph (1)(f) add–

"(g) personal independence payment.";

(b) after paragraph (1)(g) add–

"(h) universal credit.";

(c) after paragraph (1B)(d) add–

"(e) personal independence payment.";

(d) after paragraph (1B)(e) add–

"(f) universal credit.".

(3) After regulation 106 insert–

"Recovery by deduction from earnings

106A.–(1) Any overpayment which is recoverable by virtue of regulation 100 may be recovered by a relevant authority by deduction from the earnings of the person from whom it is recoverable.

(2) Part 6 of the Social Security (Overpayments and Recovery) Regulations 2013 applies in relation to the recovery of overpayments by deduction from the earnings of a person specified in paragraph (1) by a relevant authority as it applies to the recovery of recoverable amounts by deduction from the earnings of persons under that Part of those Regulations by an appropriate authority".

Amendment of the Housing Benefit (Persons who have attained the qualifying age for state pension credit) Regulations 2006

34.–(1) The Housing Benefit (Persons who have attained the qualifying age for state pension credit) Regulations 2006 (recovery of overpayments from prescribed benefits) are amended as follows.

(2) In regulation 86 (recovery of overpayments from prescribed benefits–

(a) after paragraph (1)(f) add–

"(g) personal independence payment.";

(b) after paragraph (1)(g) add–

"(h) universal credit.";

(c) after paragraph (1B)(d) add–

"(e) personal independence payment.";

(d) after paragraph (1B)(e) add–

"(f) universal credit.".

(3) After regulation 87 insert–

"Recovery by deduction from earnings

87A.–(1) Any overpayment which is recoverable by virtue of regulation 81 may be recovered by a relevant authority by deduction from the earnings of the person from whom it is recoverable.

(2) Part 6 of the Social Security (Overpayments and Recovery) Regulations 2013 applies in relation to the recovery of overpayments by deduction from the earnings of a person specified in paragraph (1) by a relevant authority as it applies to the recovery of recoverable amounts by deduction from the earnings of persons under that Part of those Regulations by an appropriate authority.".

SCHEDULE 1

Regulation 18

Exemption for existing micro-businesses and new businessess

Micro-businesses

1. A micro-business is a business that has fewer than 10 employees (see paragraphs 6 to 8).

Existing micro-businesses

2. An existing micro-business is a business that was a micro-business immediately before 8th April 2013.

New businesses

3.–(1) A new business is a business which a person, or a number of persons, ("P") begins to carry on during the period beginning on 8th April 2013 and ending on 31st March 2014.

(2) But a business is not a new business if–

(a) P has, at any time during the period of 6 months ending immediately before the date on which P begins to carry on the business, carried on another business consisting of the activities of which the business consists (or most of them); or

(b) P carries on the business as a result of a transfer (within the meaning of sub-paragraph (3)).

(3) P carries on a business as a result of a transfer if P begins to carry on the business on another person ceasing to carry on the activities of which it consists (or most of them) in consequence of arrangements involving P and the other person.

(4) For this purpose, P is to be taken to begin to carry on a business on another person ceasing to carry on such activities if–

(a) P begins to carry on the business otherwise than in partnership on such activities ceasing to be carried on by persons in partnership; or

(b) P is a number of persons in partnership who begin to carry on the business on such activities ceasing to be carried on–

(i) by a person, or a number of persons, otherwise than in partnership;

(ii) by persons in partnership who do not consist only of all the persons who constitute P; or

(iii) partly as mentioned in paragraph (i) and partly as mentioned in paragraph (ii).

(5) P is not to be regarded as beginning to carry on a business for the purposes of sub-paragraph (1) if–

(a) before P begins to carry on the business, P is a party to arrangements under which P may (at any time during the period beginning on 8th April 2013 and ending on 31st March 2014) carry on, as part of the business, activities carried on by any other person; and

(b) the business would have been prevented by sub-paragraph (2)(b) from being a new business if–

(i) P had begun to carry on the activities when beginning to carry on the business; and

(ii) the other person had at that time ceased to carry them on.

(6) "Arrangements" includes an agreement, understanding, scheme, transaction or series of transactions (whether or not legally enforceable).

The exemption period: existing micro-businesses

4.–(1) This paragraph defines the exemption period in relation to an existing micro-business.

(2) The exemption period starts on 8th April 2013 and ends on the day after a grace period in relation to the business ends, if the grace period is one in which the business grows (see paragraphs 5 and 6).

(3) The following are grace periods in relation to a business for the purposes of this paragraph–

(a) the 6-month period that starts with the first day after 8th April 2013 on which the business has 10 or more employees;

(b) the 6-month period that starts after the end of a grace period (the "earlier grace period") that is not one in which the business grows, in accordance with sub-paragraph (4) or (5).

(4) If the business has 10 or more employees on the day after the end of the earlier grace period, the next grace period starts on that day.

(5) If the business has fewer than 10 employees on that day, the next grace period starts on the next day on which the business has 10 or more employees.

Grace periods in which business grows

5.–(1) For the purposes of this Schedule, a grace period is one in which a business grows if A is greater than B, where–

(a) A is the number of days in the grace period when the business has 10 or more employees; and

(b) B is the number of days in the grace period when the business has fewer than 10 employees.

Number of employees of a business

6. For the purposes of this Schedule, the number of employees of a business is calculated as follows–

$$\frac{TH}{37.5}$$

where TH is the total number of hours per week for which all the employees of the business are contracted to work.

Employees of a business

7. For the purposes of this Schedule, the employees of a business are the persons who are employed for the purposes of the business in connection with any of the activities of which the business consists.

Employees

8.–(1) In this Schedule, "employee" means an individual who has entered into, or works under, a contract of employment.

(2) In sub-paragraph (1) "contract of employment" means a contract of service, whether express or implied, and (if it is express) whether oral or in writing.

Franchises

9. For the purposes of this Schedule, a business that is carried on pursuant to a franchise agreement is treated as part of the business of the franchisor (and not as a separate business carried on by the franchisee).

SCHEDULE 2

Regulation 20(2)

Amounts to be deducted by employers

TABLE A:

WHERE EARNINGS ARE PAID WEEKLY

AMOUNT OF NET EARNINGS	DEDUCTION (PER CENT. OF NET EARNINGS)
Less than £100	Nil
Exceeding £100 but not exceeding £160	3
Exceeding £160 but not exceeding £220	5
Exceeding £220 but not exceeding £270	7
Exceeding £270 but not exceeding £375	11
Exceeding £375 but not exceeding £520	15
Exceeding £520	20

TABLE B:

WHERE EARNINGS ARE PAID MONTHLY

AMOUNT OF NET EARNINGS	DEDUCTION (PER CENT. OF NET EARNINGS)
Less than £430	Nil
Exceeding £430 but not exceeding £690	3
Exceeding £690 but not exceeding £950	5
Exceeding £950 but not exceeding £1,160	7
Exceeding £1,160 but not exceeding £1,615	11
Exceeding £1,615 but not exceeding £2,240	15
Exceeding £2,240	20

The Social Security (Loss of Benefit) (Amendment) Regulations 2013

(SI 2013 No.385)

Made	*25th February 2013*
Coming into force in accordance with regulation 1(2)	

The Secretary of State for Work and Pensions makes the following Regulations in exercise of the powers conferred by sections 6B(5A), (6), (7)(c), (8), (9), (11) and (14), 7(2A), (3), (4)(c), (4A), (4B) and (6), 8(4)(c), 9(2), (2A), (3), (4)(c), (4A) and (4B), 10(1) and 11(1) of the Social Security Fraud Act 2001 and section 189(4) to (6) of the Social Security Administration Act 1992 ("the Administration Act"). In accordance with section 173(1)(b) of the Administration Act, the Secretary of State has obtained the agreement of the Social Security Advisory Committee that proposals in respect of these Regulations should not be referred to it.

A draft of these Regulations has been laid before, and approved by resolution of, each House of Parliament in accordance with section 11(3) of the Social Security Fraud Act 2001.

Citation and commencement

1.–(1) These Regulations may be cited as the Social Security (Loss of Benefit)(Amendment) Regulations 2013.

(2) They come into force–

(a) for the purposes of the provisions specified in paragraph (3), on 29th April 2013;

(b) for the purposes of regulations 3(f), 11(2) and 12, on 8th April 2013;

(c) for all other purposes, on 1st April 2013.

(3) The specified provisions are–

(a) regulation 3(d), (e) and (g);

(b) regulation 4(3), (6) and (7);

(c) regulation 5(3), (5)(b) and (6);

(d)-(e) [Omitted]

Amendment of the Social Security (Loss of Benefit) Regulations 2001

2. The Social Security (Loss of Benefit) Regulations 2001 are amended as follows.

Amendment of regulation 1(2)

3. In regulation 1(2) (interpretation)–

(a) before the definition of "the Act" insert–

"the 2007 Act" means the Welfare Reform Act 2007;";

"the 2012 Act" means the Welfare Reform Act 2012;";

(b) after the definition of "the Act" insert–

"the Administration Act" means the Social Security Administration Act 1992;";

(c) after the definition of "the Benefits Act" insert–

"the ESA Regulations" means the Employment and Support Allowance Regulations2008;";

(d) after the definition of "the Jobseeker's Allowance Regulations" insert–

"the UC Regulations" means the Universal Credit Regulations 2013;";

"assessment period" has the same meaning as in the UC Regulations;";

(e) after the definition of "disqualification period" insert–

"income-based jobseeker's allowance" means an income-based allowance under the Jobseekers Act as it has effect apart from the amendments made by Part 1 of Schedule 14 to the 2012 Act (to remove references to an income-based allowance);";

"income-related employment and support allowance" means an income-related allowance under the Part 1 of the 2007 Act as it has effect apart from the amendments made by Schedule 3 and Part 1 of Schedule 14 to the 2012 Act (to remove references to an income-related allowance);";

"joint claimant" means each of joint claimants as defined in section 40 of the 2012 Act;";

(f) after the definition of "pay day" insert–

"personal independence payment" means the allowance under Part 4 of the 2012 Act;";

(g) after the definition of "relevant authority" add–

"universal credit" means the benefit payable under Part 1 of the 2012 Act.".

Amendment of regulation 1A

4.–(1) Regulation 1A (disqualification period: section 6B(11) of the Act) is amended as follows.

(2) At the end of paragraph (2)(a) add "other than a benefit to which paragraph (5A) applies".

(3) At the end of paragraph (2)(a) add "or universal credit".

(4) After paragraph (5) insert–

"(5A) This paragraph applies where on the determination day the offender or, as the case may be, the offender's family member is in receipt of a sanctionable benefit which is neither payable wholly in advance nor wholly in arrears and no other sanctionable benefit.".

(5) In paragraph (6), for "neither paragraph (2) nor paragraph (4) applies" substitute "paragraph (5A) applies or where there is no sanctionable benefit payable on the determination day".

(6) After paragraph (6) insert–

"(6A) Paragraph (6B) applies where, on the determination day, the offender or, as the case may be, the offender's family member is in receipt of universal credit.

(6B) Where this paragraph applies, DQ-day is–

(a) if the first day after the end of the period of 28 days beginning with the determination day is the first day of an assessment period, that day;

(b) if the first day after the end of the period of 28 days beginning with the determination day is not the first day of an assessment period, the first day of the next assessment period after that day.".

(7) In paragraph (7)–

(a) in sub-paragraph (a), after "paragraph (2)" insert "or (6A)";

(b) in sub-paragraph (b)–

(i) for "that paragraph" substitute "those paragraphs";

(ii) after "paragraph (3)" insert "or (6B)".

Amendment of regulation 2

5.–(1) Regulation 2 (disqualification period: section 7(6) of the Act) is amended as follows.

(2) At the end of paragraph (2)(a), add "other than a benefit to which paragraph (5A) applies".

(3) At the end of paragraph (2)(a), add "or universal credit".

(4) After paragraph (5) insert–

"(5A) This paragraph applies where on the determination day the offender or, as the case may be, the offender's family member is in receipt of a sanctionable benefit which is neither payable wholly in advance nor wholly in arrears and no other sanctionable benefit.".

(5) In paragraph (6)–

(a) for "neither paragraph (2) nor paragraph (4) applies" substitute "paragraph (5A) applies or where there is no sanctionable benefit payable on the determination day";

(b) at the beginning of sub-paragraph (c) insert "universal credit,".

(6) After paragraph (6) insert–

"(6A) Paragraph (6B) applies where on the determination day, the offender or, as the case may be, the offender's family member is in receipt of universal credit.

(6B) Where this paragraph applies, DQ-day is–

(a) if the first day after the end of the period of 28 days beginning with the determination day is the first day of an assessment period, that day;

(b) if the first day after the end of the period of 28 days beginning with the determination day is not the first day of an assessment period, the first day of the next assessment period after that day.".

(7) In paragraph (7), after "this regulation" insert "but except where paragraph (8) applies".

(8) After paragraph (7) add–

"(8) Where the date of the conviction of the offender for the benefit offence in the later proceedings is on or after 1st April 2013 and on the determination day–

(a) paragraph (2) or (6A) applies in the case of an offender or, as the case may be, an offender's family member; but

(b) that person ceases to be in receipt of a benefit referred to in those paragraphs before the first day of the disqualification period that would apply by virtue of paragraph (3) or (6B),

DQ-day is the first day after the end of the period of 28 days beginning with the determination day.".

Insertion of regulation 2A

6. After regulation 2 insert–

"**Prescribed offences: section 6B(14)(b) of the Act**

2A.–(1) Paragraphs (2) to (4) prescribe offences which are relevant offences for the purpose of sections 6B and 7 of the Act where section 6B(14)(b)(i), (ii) or (iii) of the Act applies.

(2) In England and Wales, offences under–

(a) section 8 of the Accessories and Abettors Act 1861;

(b) section 1 of the Criminal Law Act 1977;

(c) section 1, 3, 4 or 5 of the Forgery and Counterfeiting Act 1981;

(d) section 6 or 7 of the Fraud Act 2006; and

(e) section 44, 45 or 46 of the Serious Crime Act 2007.

(3) In England, Wales or Scotland, offences under–

(a) section 182 of the Administration Act;

(b) section 327, 328 or 329 of the Proceeds of Crime Act 2002; and

(c) section 4, 5 or 6 of the Identity Documents Act 2010.

(4) In Scotland–

(a) the common law offences of–

(i) conspiracy to defraud;

(ii) embezzlement;

(iii) fraud;

(iv) fraudulent scheme; and

(v) uttering;

(b) offences under–

(i) section 44 of the Criminal Law (Consolidation) (Scotland) Act 1995;

(ii) section 28 or 30 of the Criminal Justice and Licensing (Scotland) Act 2010 ("the 2010 Act"); and

(c) offences to which section 29 of the 2010 Act (offences aggravated by connection with serious organised crime) applies.

(5) Paragraphs (6) and (7) prescribe offences which are relevant offences for the purpose of sections 6B and 7 of the Act where section 6B(14)(b)(i) or (ii) of the Act applies.

(6) In England and Wales, offences under section 1 of the Fraud Act 2006.

(7) In England, Wales or Scotland, offences under–

(a) section 111A of the Administration Act;

(b) section 35 of the Tax Credits Act 2002.".

The Personal Independence Payment (Supplementary Provisions and Consequential Amendments) Regulations 2013

(SI 2013 No.388)

Made	*25th February2013*
Laid before Parliament	*4th March 2013*
Coming into force in accordance with regulations 2 and 3	

The Secretary of State for Work and Pensions makes the following Regulations in exercise of the powers conferred by sections 92(1) and (2) and 94(1) of the Welfare Reform Act 2012.

These Regulations contain only regulations made by virtue of, or consequential upon, Part 4 of the Welfare Reform Act 2012 and are made before the end of the period of 6 months beginning with the coming into force of those provisions.

Citation and commencement

1. These Regulations may be cited as the Personal Independence Payment (Supplementary Provisions and Consequential Amendments) Regulations 2013.

2. Except as specified in regulation 3, they come into force on 8th April 2013.

3. *[Omitted]*

Extent and application

4. Subject to regulations 5 to 7, these Regulations extend and apply to England and Wales, Scotland and Northern Ireland.

5. The amendments made by paragraphs 4 to 11, 13, 15 to 17, 19 and 21 to 51 of the Schedule have the same extent and application as the provisions amended by those paragraphs.

6.-7. *[Omitted]*

Supplementary provisions and consequential amendments

8. The Schedule has effect.

SCHEDULE

Regulation 8

Personal independence payment: supplementary provisions and consequential amendments

PART 1

Supplementary provisions

Amendment of the Local Government Finance Act 1992

7.–(1) The Local Government Finance Act 1992 is amended as follows.

(2) In section 13 (reduced amounts), in subsection (10)–

(a) the text from "an order" to the end becomes paragraph (a); and

(b) after that paragraph insert–

"; or

(b) regulations made, or falling to be made, under Part 4 of the Welfare Reform Act 2012.".

(3) In section 80 (reduced amounts), in subsection (10)–

(a) the text from "an order" to the end becomes paragraph (a); and

(b) after that paragraph insert–

"; or

(b) regulations made, or falling to be made, under Part 4 of the Welfare Reform Act 2012.".

(4) *[Omitted]*

Amendment of the Housing Benefit Regulations 2006

36.–(1) The Housing Benefit Regulations 2006 are amended as follows.

(2) In regulation 2 (interpretation), in paragraph (1)–

(a) in the appropriate places insert–

"the 2012 Act" means the Welfare Reform Act 2012;";
"personal independence payment" means personal independence payment under Part 4 of the 2012 Act;";

(b) in the definition of "the benefit Acts" after "the Jobseekers Act" insert ", Part 4 of the 2012 Act"; and

(c) in the definition of "person who requires overnight care"–

(i) omit "or" at the end of sub-paragraph (a)(ii);

(ii) after sub-paragraph (a)(ii) insert–

"(iia) is in receipt of the daily living component of personal independence payment in accordance with section 78 of the 2012 Act; or"; and

(iii) in sub-paragraph (a)(iii) for "or (ii)" substitute ", (ii) or (iia)".

(3) In regulation 28 (treatment of child care charges)–

(a) after paragraph (11)(d)(vii) insert–

"(viii) personal independence payment;";

(b) omit "or" at the end of paragraph (13)(b); and

(c) after paragraph (13)(c) insert–

"; or

(d) in respect of whom personal independence payment is payable, or would be payable but for regulations made under section 86(1) (hospital in-patients) of the 2012 Act".

(4) In regulation 74 (non-dependant deductions)–

(a) omit "or" at the end of sub-paragraph (6)(b)(i);

(b) after sub-paragraph (6)(b)(ii) insert–

"or

(iii) the daily living component of personal independence payment;"; and

(c) in paragraph (9)(a) for "or disability living allowance" insert ", disability living allowance or personal independence payment".

(5) In regulation 79 (date on which change of circumstances is to take effect), in paragraph (6), after "the Act" insert "or Part 4 of the 2012 Act".

(6) In Schedule 3 (applicable amounts)–

(a) In paragraph 7(2) for "or the care component of disability living allowance at the highest or middle rate prescribed in accordance with section 72(3) of the Act" substitute "the care component of disability living allowance at the highest or middle rate prescribed in accordance with section 72(3) of the Act or the daily living component of personal independence payment at the standard or enhanced rate in accordance with section 78(3) of the 2012 Act";

(b) in paragraph 13 (additional condition for the disability premium), in sub-paragraph (1)(a)–

(i) in paragraph (i) after "disability living allowance," insert "personal independence payment,"; and

(ii) after paragraph (iii) insert–

"(iiia) would be in receipt of personal independence payment but for regulations made under section 86(1) (hospital in-patients) of the 2012 Act; or";

(c) in paragraph 14 (severe disability premium)–

(i) in sub-paragraph (2)(a)(i) for "or the care component of disability living allowance at the highest or middle rate prescribed in accordance with section 72(3) of the Act" substitute "the care component of disability living allowance at the highest or middle rate prescribed in accordance with section 72(3) of the Act or the daily living component of personal independence payment at the standard or enhanced rate in accordance with section 78(3) of the 2012 Act";

(ii) in sub-paragraph (2)(b)(i) for "or the care component of disability living allowance at the highest or middle rate prescribed in accordance with section 72(3) of the Act" substitute "the care component of disability living allowance at the highest or middle rate prescribed in accordance with section 72(3) of the Act or the daily living component of personal independence payment at the standard or enhanced rate in accordance with section 78(3) of the 2012 Act";

(iii) in sub-paragraph (2)(b)(ii) after "allowance" in each place where it appears insert "or payment";

(iv) in sub-paragraph (4)(a) for "or the care component of disability living allowance at the highest or middle rate prescribed in accordance with section 72(3) of the Act" substitute "the care component of disability living allowance at the highest or middle rate prescribed in accordance with section 72(3) of the Act or the daily living component of personal independence payment at the standard or enhanced rate in accordance with section 78(3) of the 2012 Act";

(v) after sub-paragraph (5)(b) insert–

"(c) as being in receipt of the daily living component of personal independence payment at the standard or enhanced rate in accordance with section 78 of the 2012 Act, if he would, but for regulations made under section 86(1) (hospital inpatients) of the 2012 Act, be so in receipt.";

(d) in paragraph 15 (enhanced disability premium), after sub-paragraph (1)(b) insert–

"; or

(c) the enhanced rate of the daily living component of personal independence payment is, or would, but for regulations made under section 86(1) (hospital in-patients) of the 2012 Act, be payable in respect of–

(i) the claimant; or

(ii) a member of the claimant's family, who has not attained the qualifying age for state pension credit"; and

(e) in paragraph 16 (disabled child premium), after sub-paragraph (c) insert–

"; or

(d) is a young person who is in receipt of personal independence payment or who would, but for regulations made under section 86(1) (hospital in-patients) of the 2012 Act be so in receipt, provided that the young person continues to be a member of the family".

(7) In paragraph 6 of Schedule 5 (sums to be disregarded in the calculation of income other than earnings) after "disability living allowance" insert "or personal independence payment".

Amendment of the Housing Benefit (Persons who have attained the qualifying age for state pension credit) Regulations 2006

37.–(1) The Housing Benefit (Persons who have attained the qualifying age for state pension credit) Regulations 2006 are amended as follows.

(2) In regulation 2 (interpretation), in paragraph (1)–

(a) in the appropriate places insert–

"the 2012 Act" means the Welfare Reform Act 2012;";

"personal independence payment" means personal independence payment under Part 4 of the 2012 Act;";

(b) in the definition of "the benefit Acts" after "Welfare Reform Act" insert ", Part 4 of the 2012 Act";

(c) in the definition of "person who requires overnight care"–

(i) omit "or" at the end of sub-paragraph (a)(ii);

(ii) after sub-paragraph (a)(ii) insert–

"(iia) is in receipt of the daily living component of personal independence payment in accordance with section 78 of the 2012 Act; or"; and

(iii) in sub-paragraph (a)(iii) for "or (ii)" substitute ", (ii) or (iia)".

(3) In regulation 29 (meaning of "income") after paragraph (1)(j)(i) insert–

"(ia) personal independence payment;".

(4) In regulation 31 (treatment of child care charges)–

(a) after paragraph (11)(d)(vii) insert–

"(viii) personal independence payment;";

(b) omit "or" at the end of paragraph (13)(b); and
(c) after paragraph (13)(c) insert–

"; or
(d) in respect of whom personal independence payment is payable, or would be payable but for regulations made under section 86(1) (hospital in-patients) of the 2012 Act".

(5) In regulation 55 (non-dependant deductions)–
(a) omit "or" at the end of paragraph (6)(b)(i);
(b) after paragraph (6)(b)(ii) insert–

"; or
(iii) the daily living component of personal independence payment"; and

(c) in paragraph (10)(a) for "or disability living allowance" substitute ", disability living allowance or personal independence payment".

(6) In regulation 59 (date on which change of circumstances is to take effect), in paragraph (6), after "the Act" insert "or Part 4 of the 2012 Act".

(7) In Schedule 3 (applicable amounts)–
(a) for paragraph 5(2) substitute–

"(2) For the purposes of the carer premium under paragraph 9, a person shall be treated as being in receipt of a carer's allowance under section 70 of the Act by virtue of subparagraph (1)(a) only if and for so long as the person in respect of whose care the allowance has been claimed remains in receipt of–
(a) attendance allowance;
(b) the care component of disability living allowance at the highest or middle rate prescribed in accordance with section 72(3) of the Act; or
(c) the daily living component of personal independence payment at the standard or enhanced rate in accordance with section 78(3) of the 2012 Act.";

(b) in paragraph 6 (severe disability premium)–
(i) in sub-paragraph (2)(a)(i) for "or the care component of disability living allowance at the highest or middle rate prescribed in accordance with section 72(3) of the Act" substitute ", the care component of disability living allowance at the highest or middle rate prescribed in accordance with section 72(3) of the Act or the daily living component of personal independence payment at the standard or enhanced rate in accordance with section 78(3) of the 2012 Act";
(ii) in sub-paragraph (2)(b)(i) for "or the care component of disability living allowance at the highest or middle rate prescribed in accordance with section 72(3) of the Act" substitute ", the care component of disability living allowance at the highest or middle rate prescribed in accordance with section 72(3) of the Act or the daily living component of personal independence payment at the standard or enhanced rate in accordance with section 78(3) of the 2012 Act";
(iii) in sub-paragraph (2)(b)(ii) after "allowance" in each place where it appears insert "or payment";
(iv) in sub-paragraph (6)(a) for "or the care component of disability living allowance at the highest or middle rate prescribed in accordance with section 72(3) of the Act" substitute ", the care component of disability living allowance at the highest or middle rate prescribed in accordance with section 72(3) of the Act or the daily living component of personal independence payment at the standard or enhanced rate in accordance with section 78(3) of the 2012 Act";
(v) after sub-paragraph (7)(b) insert–

"(c) as being in receipt of the daily living component of personal independence payment at the standard or enhanced rate in accordance with section 78 of the 2012 Act, if he would, but for regulations made under section 86(1) (hospital inpatients) of the 2012 Act, be so in receipt.";

(c) in paragraph 7 (enhanced disability premium) for sub-paragraph (1) substitute–

"(1) Subject to sub-paragraph (2), the condition is that–
(a) the care component of disability living allowance is, or would, but for a suspension of benefit in accordance with regulations under section 113(2) of the Act or but for an abatement as a consequence of hospitalisation, be payable at the highest rate prescribed under section 72(3) of the Act; or

(b) the daily living component of personal independence payment is, or would, but for regulations made under section 86(1) (hospital in-patients) of the 2012 Act, be payable at the enhanced rate under section 78(2) of the 2012 Act;

in respect of a child or young person who is a member of the claimant's family."; and

(d) in paragraph 8 (disabled child premium), after sub-paragraph (c) insert–

"; or

(d) is a young person who is in receipt of personal independence payment or who would, but for regulations made under section 86(1) (hospital in-patients) of the 2012 Act be so in receipt, provided that the young person continues to be a member of the family".

(8) In paragraph 5(1)(a) of Schedule 4 (sums disregarded from claimant's earnings)–

(a) omit "or" at the end of paragraph (vii); and

(b) after paragraph (vii) insert–

"(viii) personal independence payment; or".

(9) After paragraph 21(2)(b) of Schedule 6 (capital to be disregarded) insert–

"(ba) personal independence payment;".

Amendment to the Social Security (Information-sharing in relation to Welfare Services etc.) Regulations 2012

48. In regulation 4 (prescribed benefits) of the Social Security (Information-sharing in relation to Welfare Services etc.) Regulations 2012–

(a) omit "and" at the end of sub-paragraph (e); and

(b) after sub-paragraph (f) insert–

"; and

(g) personal independence payment under Part 4 of the 2012 Act".

Amendment to the Benefit Cap (Housing Benefit) Regulations 2012

51. In regulation 2 (amendment of the Housing Benefit Regulations 2006) of the Benefit Cap (Housing Benefit) Regulations 2012 in paragraph (5), in regulation 75F inserted by those Regulations–

(a) after sub-paragraph (e) insert–

"(ea) the claimant, the claimant's partner or a young person for whom the claimant or the claimant's partner is responsible, is receiving a personal independence payment;";

(b) in sub-paragraph (f) for "or (e)" substitute ", (e) or (ea)"; and

(c) after sub-paragraph (f)(iii) insert–

"(iv) that payment is not payable in accordance with regulations made under section 85 (care home residents) or section 86(1) (hospital in-patients) of the Welfare Reform Act 2012;".

The Social Security (Miscellaneous Amendments) Regulations 2013

(SI 2013 No.443)

Made	*25th February2013*
Laid before Parliament	*4th March 2013*
Coming into force in accordance with regulation 1	

The Secretary of State for Work and Pensions makes the following Regulations in exercise of the powers conferred by sections 123(1)(d), 135(1), 136(1), 136A(3), 137(1) and (2)(h) and 175(1), (3) and (4) of the Social Security Contributions and Benefits Act 1992, sections 5(1)(p) and (2) and 189(1), (4) and (5) of the Social Security Administration Act 1992, sections 4(5), 8(2), 12(4), 13(2), 19A(4), 19B(2) and (4), 35(1) and 36(2) and (4) of the Jobseekers Act 1995, sections 10(6), 79(1) and 84 of the Social Security Act 1998, sections 2(3)(b), 15(3) and (6), 17(1) and 19(1) of the State Pension Credit Act 2002, sections 17(1) and (3)(b), 24(1) and 25(2), (3) and (5)(a) of the Welfare Reform Act 2007, and sections 92(1) and (4) and 94(1) of the Welfare Reform Act 2012.

In accordance with section 173(1)(b) of the Social Security Administration Act 1992, the Secretary of State has obtained the agreement of the Social Security Advisory Committee that proposals in respect of these Regulations should not be referred to it.

In respect of the provisions in these Regulations relating to housing benefit, the Secretary of State has consulted with organisations appearing to him to be representative of the authorities concerned.

Citation and commencement

1.–(1) These Regulations may be cited as the Social Security (Miscellaneous Amendments) Regulations 2013 and subject to paragraphs (2) and (3) come into force on 2nd April 2013.

(2)-(3) *[Omitted]*

Amendments to the Housing Benefit Regulations 2006

7.–(1) The Housing Benefit Regulations 2006 are amended as follows.

(2) After the definition of "local housing allowance" in regulation 2(1) (interpretation), insert–

"local welfare provision" means occasional financial or other assistance given by a local authority, the Scottish Ministers or the Welsh Ministers, or a person authorised to exercise any function of, or provide a service to, them, to or in respect of individuals for the purpose of–

(a) meeting, or helping to meet, an immediate short term need–
  (i) arising out of an exceptional event, or exceptional circumstances; and
  (ii) that requires to be met in order to avoid a risk to the well-being of an individual; or

(b) enabling individuals to establish or maintain a settled home, where those individuals have been or, without the assistance, might otherwise be–
  (i) in prison, hospital, a residential care establishment or other institution; or
  (ii) homeless or otherwise living an unsettled way of life;".

(3) In regulation 7 (circumstances in which a person is or is not to be treated as occupying a dwelling as his home)–

(a) in paragraph (8)(c)(ii), after "pending", insert "local welfare provision or";

(b) for paragraph (16)(c)(i), substitute–

"(i) a person to whom paragraph (16A) applies;"; and

(c) after paragraph (16), insert–

"(16A) This paragraph applies to a person ("P") who is–
(a) detained in custody on remand pending trial;
(b) detained pending sentence upon conviction; or
(c) as a condition of bail required to reside–
(i) in a dwelling, other than a dwelling P occupies as P's home; or
(ii) in premises approved under section 13 of the Offender Management Act 2007,

and who is not also detained in custody following sentence upon conviction.".

(4) In Schedule 3 (applicable amounts)–

(a) in Part 5 (the components) for paragraph 21(a) substitute–

"**21.**–(1) Subject to paragraph 22, the claimant is entitled to one, but not both, of the components in paragraph 23 or 24 if–
(a) the claimant or the claimant's partner has made a claim for employment and support allowance;
(b) the Secretary of State has determined that the claimant or the claimant's partner–
(i) has limited capability for work or limited capability for work-related activity; or
(ii) is to be treated as having limited capability for work other than by virtue of regulation 30 of the Employment and Support Allowance Regulations (conditions for treating a claimant as having limited capability for work until a determination about limited capability for work has been made); and
(c) one of the following applies–
(i) the assessment phase as defined in section 24(2) of the Welfare Reform Act (interpretation) has ended;
(ii) regulation 7 of the Employment and Support Allowance Regulations (circumstances where the condition that the assessment phase has ended before entitlement to the support component or the work-related activity component arises does not apply) applies; or
(iii) the conditions in sub-paragraph (2) apply.
(2) The conditions referred to in sub-paragraph (1)(c)(iii) are–
(a) neither the claimant nor the claimant's partner is entitled to an employment and support allowance;
(b) either is or both are entitled to be credited with earnings equal to the lower earnings limit then in force under regulation 8B(2)(a)(iv) of the Social Security (Credits) Regulations 1975 (credits for incapacity for work or limited capability for work); and
(c) paragraph (1)(c)(i) or (ii) would have applied to the claimant or the claimant's partner (or both) had they been entitled to an employment and support allowance."; and

(b) in Part 7 (transitional addition) in paragraph 28(b)–
(i) in sub-paragraph (1)(c), after "the relevant person", insert "satisfies the requirements of paragraph 27(1) or";
(ii) in sub-paragraph (3)(c), after "relevant person" insert "no longer satisfying the requirements of paragraph 27(1) or".

(5) In Schedule 5 (sums to be disregarded in the calculation of income other earnings)–
(a) after paragraph 31, insert–

"**31A.** Any local welfare provision."; and

(b) in paragraph 41(c), after "section 13" insert ", section 13A".
(6) In Schedule 6 (capital to be disregarded)–
(a) after paragraph 20, insert–

"**20A.** Any local welfare provision."; and

(b) in paragraph 37, for "or, as the case may be,", substitute ", section 13A or".

Amendments to the Housing Benefit (Persons who have attained the qualifying age for state pension credit) Regulations 2006

8.–(1) The Housing Benefit (Persons who have attained the qualifying age for state pension credit) Regulations 2006 are amended as follows.

(2) After the definition of "local housing allowance" in regulation 2(1) (interpretation), insert–

"local welfare provision" means occasional financial or other assistance given by a local authority, the Scottish Ministers or the Welsh Ministers, or a person authorised to exercise any function of, or provide a service to, them, to or in respect of individuals for the purpose of–

(a) meeting, or helping to meet, an immediate short term need–
   (i) arising out of an exceptional event, or exceptional circumstances; and
   (ii) that requires to be met in order to avoid a risk to the well-being of an individual; or

(b) enabling individuals to establish or maintain a settled home, where those individuals have been or, without the assistance, might otherwise be–
   (i) in prison, hospital, a residential care establishment or other institution; or
   (ii) homeless or otherwise living an unsettled way of life;".

(3) In regulation 7 (circumstances in which a person is or is not to be treated as occupying a dwelling as his home)–

(a) in paragraph (8)(c)(ii), after "pending", insert "local welfare provision or";

(b) for paragraph (16)(c)(i), substitute–

"(i) a person to whom paragraph (16A) applies;"; and

(c) after paragraph (16), insert–

"(16A) This paragraph applies to a person ("P") who is–

(a) detained in custody on remand pending trial;

(b) detained pending sentence upon conviction; or

(c) as a condition of bail required to reside–
   (i) in a dwelling, other than a dwelling P occupies as P's home; or
   (ii) in premises approved under section 13 of the Offender Management Act 2007,

and who is not also detained in custody following sentence upon conviction.".

(4) In Schedule 6 (capital to be disregarded)–

(a) in paragraph 21–
   (i) after sub-paragraph (1)(e), insert–

"(f) by way of local welfare provision including arrears and payments in lieu of local welfare provision.";

   (ii) omit "or" at the end of sub-paragraph (2)(l)(d); and
   (iii) after sub-paragraph (2)(m) add–

"(n) social fund payments"; and

(b) after paragraph 26D, insert–

"**26E.** Any payment in consequence of a reduction of council tax under section 13, 13A or 80 of the Local Government Finance Act 1992 (reduction of liability for council tax), but only for a period of 52 weeks from the date of the receipt of the payment.".

The Social Security (Information-sharing in relation to Welfare Services etc.) Amendment and Prescribed Bodies Regulations 2013

(SI 2013 No.454)

Made	*27th February 2013*
Laid before Parliament	*5th March 2013*
Coming into force	*1st April 2013*

The Secretary of State for Work and Pensions makes the following Regulations in exercise of the powers conferred by sections 131(1), (2), (3), (11) and (12), 132(8) and 133(1) and (2) of the Welfare Reform Act 2012.

Citation, commencement and interpretation

1.–(1) These Regulations may be cited as the Social Security (Information-sharing in relation to Welfare Services etc.) Amendment and Prescribed Bodies Regulations 2013.

(2) They come into force on 1st April 2013.

(3) In these Regulations "the 2012 Act" means the Welfare Reform Act 2012.

Prescription of Scottish bodies and Welsh bodies

2.–(1) The following are prescribed as Scottish bodies for the purpose of paragraph (d) of the definition of that term in section 131(12) of the 2012 Act–

(a) the Scottish Ministers;

(b) a person authorised to exercise any function of the Scottish Ministers relating to welfare services;

(c) a person providing to the Scottish Ministers services relating to welfare services.

(2) The following are prescribed as Welsh bodies for the purpose of paragraph (d) of the definition of that term in section 131(12) of the 2012 Act–

(a) the Welsh Ministers;

(b) a person authorised to exercise any function of the Welsh Ministers relating to welfare services;

(c) a person providing to the Welsh Ministers services relating to welfare services.

Amendment of the Social Security (Information-sharing in relation to Welfare Services etc.) Regulations 2012

3.–(1) The Social Security (Information-sharing in relation to Welfare Services etc.) Regulations 2012 are amended as follows.

(2) In regulation 2 (interpretation)–

(a)–(b) [Omitted]

(c) after the definition of "landlord" insert–

"local welfare provision" means occasional financial or other assistance given by a local authority, the Scottish Ministers or the Welsh Ministers, or a person authorised to exercise any function of theirs or providing a service to them, to or in respect of individuals for the purpose of–

(a) meeting, or helping to meet, an immediate short term need–

(i) arising out of an exceptional event or exceptional circumstances; and

(ii) that requires to be met in order to avoid a risk to the well-being of an individual; or

(b) enabling individuals to establish or maintain a settled home, where those individuals have been or, without the assistance, might otherwise be–

(i) in prison, hospital, a residential care establishment or other institution; or

(ii) homeless or otherwise living an unsettled way of life;";

(d) *[Omitted]*
(e) in the definition of "the troubled families programme", for "the troubled families programme" means the programme of assistance provided by local authorities" substitute "troubled families programme" means any programme of assistance provided by a local authority";
(f) after the definition of "troubled families programme" (as amended by the preceding subparagraph) insert–

"universal credit" means universal credit under Part 1 of the 2012 Act.".

(3) In regulation 5 (supply of relevant information by the Secretary of State)–
(a) for paragraph (1)(a) substitute–

"(a) determining a person's eligibility or continued eligibility for–
(i) a disabled person's badge;
(ii) assistance under the healthy start scheme; or
(iii) local welfare provision;";

(b) omit "and" at the end of paragraph (1)(c);
(c) for paragraph (1)(d) substitute–

"(d) where the qualifying person is a local authority in England–
(i) identifying households eligible for support under a troubled families programme;
(ii) providing appropriate types of advice, support and assistance to members of such households under such programmes; and
monitoring and evaluating such programmes;";

(d) after paragraph (1)(d) add–

"(e) discharging any functions under Part 7 of the Housing Act 1996 or (in Scotland) Part 2 of the Housing (Scotland) Act 1987; and
(f) identifying, and providing appropriate types of advice, support and assistance to, persons in receipt of a relevant social security benefit who are or may be affected by–
(i) the benefit cap;
(ii) regulations relating to under-occupation.".

(4) In regulation 6 (holding purposes)–
(a) for paragraph (1)(a) substitute–

"(a) determining a person's eligibility or continued eligibility for–
(i) a disabled person's badge;
(ii) assistance under the healthy start scheme;
(iii) housing support services; or
(iv) local welfare provision;";

(b) for paragraph (1)(d) substitute–

"(d) where the qualifying person is a local authority in England, a person providing services to a local authority in England relating to a troubled families programme, or a person who falls within regulation 10(1)(b)–
(i) identifying households eligible for support under a troubled families programme;
(ii) providing appropriate types of advice, support and assistance to members of such households under such programmes; and
monitoring and evaluating such programmes;";

(c) in paragraph (1)(g) and (l) for "housing benefit claimant" substitute "person in receipt of a relevant social security benefit";
(d) in paragraph (1)(h) and (i) for "housing benefit claimants" substitute "persons in receipt of a relevant social security benefit";
(e) after paragraph (1)(o) add–

"(p) identifying the amount of housing costs included in an award of universal credit by reference to the local housing allowance.".

(5) In regulation 7 (using purposes connected with welfare services and housing benefit)–
(a) in paragraph (1) for "purpose listed in regulation 6(d)" substitute "purposes listed in regulation 6(1)(a)(ii), (iv) or (d)";
(b) for paragraph (3)(a) substitute–

"(a) the purposes referred to in regulation 6(1)(a)(i) or (iii), (b), (c), (e), (h) or (i);";

(c) in paragraph (3)(c) for "housing benefit claimant" substitute "person in receipt of a relevant social security benefit".
(6) In regulation 8 (using purposes connected with the troubled families programme)–
(a) in the heading, and in paragraph (3), for "the troubled families programme" substitute "a troubled families programme";
(b) in paragraph (1)–
(i) after "England" add "or a person who falls within regulation 10(1)(b)";
(ii) for ''6(d)" substitute ''6(1)(d)";
(iii) for ''6(i)" substitute ''6(1)(i)";
(c) at the end of paragraph (4) add "or a person who falls within regulation 10(1)(b).";
(d) after paragraph (4) add–

"(5) The references in regulations 8(1) and (4) to a local authority in England include references to a person providing services to a local authority in England relating to a troubled families programme.''.

(7) In regulation 9(1) for ''6(f)" substitute ''6(1)(f)".
(8) In regulation 9(3)(a) and (b) for "housing benefit claimants" substitute "persons in receipt of a relevant social security benefit".
(9) After regulation 9 (using purposes connected with under-occupation and benefit cap) insert–

"Using purposes connected with the healthy start scheme
9A. *[Omitted]*

Using purposes connected with local welfare provision
9B.–(1) This regulation applies to relevant information held by a qualifying person listed in regulation 10(1)(d) or section 131(11)(a) to (c) of the 2012 Act for the purpose listed in regulation 6(1)(a)(iv).
(2) The purposes set out in paragraph (3) are prescribed–
(a) under section 131(3)(a) of the 2012 Act as purposes for which the information may be used by a qualifying person; and
(b) subject to regulation 11, under section 131(3)(b) of the 2012 Act as purposes for use in relation to which the information may be supplied by that qualifying person to another qualifying person.
(3) The purposes are any purposes connected with local welfare provision.

(4) This regulation permits relevant information to be supplied to another qualifying person only where that other qualifying person is listed in regulation 10(1)(d) or section 131(11)(a) to (c) of the 2012 Act.".

(10) For regulation 10 (qualifying persons) substitute–

"**10.**–(1) The following persons are prescribed as qualifying persons under section 131(11)(g) of the 2012 Act–

(a) for the purposes of regulations 6(1)(f) to (i) and 9, a social landlord;
(b) for the purposes of regulations 6(1)(d) and 8, a person who carries out activities in connection with a troubled families programme;
(c) for the purposes of regulations 5(1)(a)(ii), 6(1)(a)(ii) and 9A–
 (i) the Secretary of State for Health;
 (ii) a person providing services to the Secretary of State for Health relating to the healthy start scheme;
(d) for the purposes of regulations 5(1)(a)(iii), 6(1)(a)(iv) and 9B–
 (i) the Scottish Ministers;
 (ii) a person authorised to exercise any function of the Scottish Ministers relating to local welfare provision;
 (iii) a person providing to the Scottish Ministers services relating to local welfare provision;
 (iv) the Welsh Ministers;
 (v) a person authorised to exercise any function of the Welsh Ministers relating to local welfare provision;
 (vi) a person providing to the Welsh Ministers services relating to local welfare provision.

(2) The provisions of section 132 of the 2012 Act (offence of unlawful disclosure) apply to–

(a) the qualifying persons listed in paragraph (1) other than the Secretary of State for Health, the Scottish Ministers and the Welsh Ministers; and
(b) any person ("A") associated with a qualifying person listed in paragraph (1)(a), (c)(i), (d)(i) or (iv) by reason of A's office or employment or otherwise.".

(11) In regulation 11(1) (excepted matters) for "6(a)" substitute "6(1)(a)(i) or (iii)".
(12) After regulation 11(1) insert–

"(1A) Regulation 9B(2)(b) does not permit relevant information held by a Welsh body or a Scottish body to be supplied by that body to another qualifying person for use in relation to any purpose connected with local welfare provision.".

(13)-(15) *[Omitted]*
(16) After regulation 15 (excepted matters) add–

"*PART 5*

Information-sharing in relation to social security benefits under section 131(2) of the 2012 act

Holding purposes

16. The purposes prescribed under section 131(2) of the 2012 Act (supply of information to the Secretary of State or service provider for purposes relating to relevant social security benefit) as purposes for which relevant information must be held by a qualifying person in order for them to supply it as set out in that subsection, are any of the following–

(a) determining whether a person occupies as their home a dwelling which falls within paragraph 4(1)(b) of Schedule 3 to the Housing Benefit and Council Tax Benefit (Consequential Provisions) Regulations 2006;

(b) determining whether a person has, or is likely to have, difficulty in managing their financial affairs;

(c) where the qualifying person is a local authority in England–

(i) identifying households eligible for support under a troubled families programme;

(ii) providing appropriate types of advice, support and assistance to members of such households under such programmes; and

(iii) monitoring and evaluating such programmes.

Prescribed purposes relating to a relevant social security benefit

17.–(1) This regulation applies to relevant information held by a qualifying person for any purpose listed in regulation 16.

(2) The purposes set out in paragraph (3) are prescribed under section 131(2) of the 2012 Act as purposes for which the information may be supplied to the Secretary of State or a person providing services to the Secretary of State.

(3) Those purposes are–

(a) in relation to the purposes prescribed in regulation 16(a) and (b), any purpose connected with the administration of universal credit;

(b) in relation to any purpose prescribed in regulation 16(c)–

(i) any purpose connected with providing appropriate types of advice, support and assistance to a person in connection with their receipt of a relevant social security benefit; and

(ii) any purpose connected with monitoring and evaluating the effect of participation in a troubled families programme on receipt of a relevant social security benefit.".

The Council Tax Benefit Abolition (Consequential Provision) Regulations 2013

(SI 2013 No.458)

Made	*28th February 2013*
Laid before Parliament	*5th March 2013*
Coming into force	*1st April 2013*

The Secretary of State for Work and Pensions makes the following Regulations in exercise of the powers conferred by section 32 of the Welfare Reform Act 2012.

Citation and commencement

1. These Regulations may be cited as the Council Tax Benefit Abolition (Consequential Provision) Regulations 2013 and come into force on 1st April 2013.

Extent and application

2.–(1) Subject to paragraph (2), each of the revocations and amendments made by these Regulations has the same extent and application as the provision revoked or amended.

(2) *[Omitted]*

Revocations

3. The provisions specified in column 1 of Schedule 1 to these Regulations are revoked to the extent specified in column 3 of that Schedule.

SCHEDULE 1

Regulation 3

Revocations

Statutory Instrument	Statutory Instrument Number	Extent of Revocation
The Discretionary Financial Assistance Regulations 2001	2001/1167	In regulation 2– (a) in paragraph (1)(a)the words, "council tax benefit or to both"; (b) in paragraph (1)(b), the words "or benefits"; (c) paragraph (3)(a). In regulation 3– (a) in sub-paragraph (c), the words "in a case where the person is entitled to housing benefit but not council tax benefit"; (b) sub-paragraphs (d) and (e). In regulation 4– (a) in sub-paragraph (a) the words, ", other than payments in respect of council tax,"; (b) sub-paragraph (b). In regulation 5(2), the words "council tax benefit or to both". In regulation 6– (a) in paragraph (1)(b)(i), the words ", as the case may be, council tax benefit"; (b) in paragraph (2), the words "or council tax benefit."
The Housing Benefit Regulations 2006	2006/213	In regulation 109(3), the words "or council tax benefit". In Schedule 5, paragraph 51.

Statutory Instrument	Statutory Instrument Number	Extent of Revocation
The Housing Benefit (Persons who have attained the qualifying age for state pension credit) Regulations 2006	2006/214	Regulation 29(1)(j)(xii). In regulation 90(3) and in paragraph 5(2) and (3) of Schedule 4, the words "or council tax benefit". In Schedule 6, in paragraph 22(4) in paragraph (a) of the definition of "official error", the words "or council tax benefit".

The Tribunal Procedure (Amendment) Rules 2013

(SI 2013 No.477)

Made	*5th March 2013*
Laid before Parliament	*6th March 2013*
Coming into force in accordance with rule 1(2)	

The Tribunal Procedure Committee has made the following Rules in exercise of the powers conferred by section 20(2) of the Social Security Act 1998 and sections 22 and 29 of, and Schedule 5 to, the Tribunals, Courts and Enforcement Act 2007, having consulted in accordance with paragraph 28(1) of that Schedule to that Act.

The Lord Chancellor has allowed the Rules in accordance with paragraph 28(3) of that Schedule to that Act

Citation and commencement

1.–(1) These Rules may be cited as the Tribunal Procedure (Amendment) Rules 2013.

(2) They come into force–

(a) for the purposes of the amendments made by rules 22 to 32 (except for rule 27), on 8th April 2013;

(b) for the purposes of the amendments made by rule 27, on 1st October 2014; and

(c) for all other purposes, on 1st April 2013.

Amendments to the Tribunal Procedure (First-tier Tribunal) (Social Entitlement Chamber) Rules 2008

22. The Tribunal Procedure (First-tier Tribunal) (Social Entitlement Chamber) Rules 2008 are amended as follows.

24. In rule 17 (withdrawal)–

(a) in paragraph (1)(a), omit "at any time before a hearing to consider the disposal of the proceedings (or, if the Tribunal disposes of the proceedings without a hearing, before that disposal),";

(b) in paragraph (3)(a), omit "under paragraph (1)(a)";

(c) for paragraph (3)(b) and the preceding ", or", substitute–

"(b) in a social security and child support case where the Tribunal has directed that notice of withdrawal shall take effect only with the Tribunal's consent; or

(c) at a hearing.";

(d) in paragraph (6), for "of an withdrawal" substitute "that a withdrawal has taken effect."

25. In rule 22 (cases in which the notice of appeal is to be sent to the Tribunal)–

(a) for paragraph (1) substitute–

"(1) This rule applies to all cases except those to which–

(a) rule 23 (cases in which the notice of appeal is to be sent to the decision maker), or

(b) rule 26 (social security and child support cases started by reference or information in writing), applies.";

(b) in paragraph (2) after sub-paragraph (b), insert a semi-colon and the following–

"(c) in appeals under the Vaccine Damage Payments Act 1979(c), at any time;

(d) in other cases–

(i) if mandatory reconsideration applies, within 1 month after the date on which the appellant was sent notice of the result of mandatory reconsideration;

(ii) if mandatory reconsideration does not apply, within the time specified in Schedule 1 to these Rules (time specified for providing notices of appeal)";

(c) in paragraph (3)–

(i) in sub-paragraph (d), after "respondent" insert "other than the decision maker", and

(ii) omit sub-paragraph (e), except for ": and";

(d) in paragraph (4)–

(i) for sub-paragraph (a), substitute–

"(a) a copy of–

(i) the notice of the result of mandatory reconsideration, in any social security and child support case to which mandatory reconsideration applies;

(ii) the decision being challenged, in any other case;";

(ii) in sub-paragraph (b), for "or can reasonably obtain" substitute "; and";

(iii) at the end of sub-paragraph (c), omit "; and";

(iv) omit sub-paragraph (d);

(e) in paragraph (6)(b), at the beginning, insert "subject to paragraph (8)";

(f) in paragraph (7)(b), for "criminal injuries compensation cases" substitute "all other";

(g) after paragraph (7), insert–

"(8) Where an appeal in a social security and child support case is not made within the time specified in paragraph (2)–

(a) it will be treated as having been made in time, unless the Tribunal directs otherwise, if it is made within not more than 12 months of the time specified and neither the decision maker nor any other respondent objects;

(b) the time for bringing the appeal may not be extended under rule 5(3)(a) by more than 12 months.

(9) For the purposes of this rule, mandatory reconsideration applies where the notice of the decision being challenged includes a statement to the effect that there is a right of appeal in relation to the decision only if the decision-maker has considered an application for the revision, reversal, review or reconsideration (as the case may be) of the decision being challenged.".

26. In rule 23 (cases in which the notice of appeal is to be sent to the decision maker), for paragraph (1) substitute–

"(1) This rule applies to social security and child support cases in which the notice of decision being challenged informs the appellant that any appeal must be sent to the decision maker.".

28. In rule 33 (notice of decisions), in paragraph (2), for "a decision which finally disposes of all issues in the proceedings (except a decision under Part 4)" substitute "a decision (other than a decision under Part 4) which finally disposes of all issues in the proceedings or of a preliminary issue dealt with following a direction under rule 5(3)(e)".

29. In rule 34 (reasons for decisions)–

(a) in paragraph (3), for "which finally disposes of all issues in the proceedings" substitute–

"which finally disposes of–

(a) all issues in the proceedings; or

(b) a preliminary issue dealt with following a direction under rule 5(3)(e).";

(b) in paragraph (4), omit "which finally disposes of all issues in the proceedings".

30. In rule 38 (application for permission to appeal)–

(a) before sub-paragraph (a) of paragraph (3), insert–

"(za) the relevant decision notice;";

(b) in sub-paragraph (a) of paragraph (3), at the end, insert–

", if the decision disposes of–

(i) all issues in the proceedings; or

(ii) subject to paragraph (3A), a preliminary issue dealt with following a direction under rule 5(3)(e);";

(c) after paragraph (3), insert–

"(3A) The Tribunal may direct that the 1 month within which a party may send or deliver an application for permission to appeal against a decision that disposes of a preliminary issue shall run from the date of the decision that disposes of all issues in the proceedings.";

(d) in paragraph (7), after "paragraph (2)" insert "in respect of a decision that disposes of proceedings or of a preliminary issue dealt with following a direction under rule 5(3)(e)".

31. In Schedule 1 (time limits for providing notices of appeal to the decision maker)–

(a) in the heading to the Schedule, omit "to the decision maker";

(b) in the second column of the first entry, for paragraph (c)(a) substitute–

"(c) if the appellant made an application for revision of the decision under–

(i)-(ii)[Omitted]

(iii) regulation 4 of the Housing Benefit and Council Tax Benefit (Decisions and Appeals) Regulations 2001;

(iv)-(v)[Omitted]

and that application was unsuccessful, 1 month after the date on which notice that the decision would not be revised was sent to the appellant.".

Amendments to the Tribunal Procedure (Upper Tribunal) Rules 2008

49. The Tribunal Procedure (Upper Tribunal) Rules 2008 are amended as follows.

50. In rule 10(3) (circumstances in which Tribunal may award costs), in paragraph (c) after "(wasted costs)" insert "and costs incurred in applying for such costs".

51. In rule 10(6) (time limit for seeking orders for costs), for sub-paragraph (b) substitute–

"(b) notice under rule 17(5) that a withdrawal which ends the proceedings has taken effect."

52. In rule 10(8)(c) (detailed assessment), after "costs or expenses" insert ", including the costs or expenses of the assessment,".

53. In rule 10, after paragraph (9) insert–

"(10) Upon making an order for the assessment of costs, the Tribunal may order an amount to be paid on account before the costs or expenses are assessed.".

54. In rule 17 (withdrawal)–

(a) in paragraph (1)(a), omit "at any time before a hearing to consider the disposal of the proceedings (or, if the Tribunal disposes of the proceedings without a hearing, before that disposal),";

(b) in paragraph (5), for "of a withdrawal" substitute "that a withdrawal has taken effect".

55. In rule 18 (notice of funding of legal services), in paragraph (a)(i)–

(a) for "funding is granted by the Legal Services Commission or" substitute "civil legal services (within the meaning of section 8 of the Legal Aid, Sentencing and Punishment of Offenders Act 2012) are provided under arrangements made for the purposes of Part 1 of that Act or by";

(b) after "a copy of the" insert "certificate or".

56. In rule 40 (decisions), in paragraph (2)–

(a) for ", a decision which finally disposes of all issues in the proceedings (except a decision under Part 7)" substitute "a decision (other than a decision under Part 7) which finally disposes of all issues in the proceedings or of a preliminary issue dealt with following a direction under rule 5(3)(e)";

(b) in sub-paragraph (a) of that paragraph, insert "Upper" before "Tribunal".

The Benefit Cap (Housing Benefit) (Amendment) Regulations 2013

(SI 2013 No.546)

Made	*8th March 2013*
Laid before Parliament	*12th March 2013*
Coming into force	*15th April 2013*

The Secretary of State for Work and Pensions makes the following Regulations in exercise of the powers conferred by sections 96(1), (4)(a) and (c) and (10) and 97(1) of the Welfare Reform Act 2012.

In accordance with section 176(1) of the Social Security Administration Act 1992, the Secretary of State has consulted with organisations appearing to him to be representative of the authorities concerned.

Citation and commencement

1. These Regulations may be cited as the Benefit Cap (Housing Benefit) (Amendment) Regulations 2013 and come into force on 15th April 2013.

Amendment of the Benefit Cap (Housing Benefit) Regulations 2012

2.–(1) The Benefit Cap (Housing Benefit) Regulations 2012 are amended as follows.

(2) In regulation 2(5), insofar as it inserts regulation 75C of the Housing Benefit Regulations 2006 (manner of calculating the amount of welfare benefits), for paragraph (2) substitute–

"(2) Where the welfare benefit is housing benefit, the relevant authority–

(a) where the dwelling is exempt accommodation within the meaning paragraph 4(10) of Schedule 3 to the Consequential Provisions Regulations, must use the amount of nil; and

(b) in any other case, must not take account of any reduction under regulation 75D and must use the amount to which the claimant would be entitled by virtue of section 130 of the Act.".

(3) In regulation 2(5), insofar as it inserts regulation 75F(1) of the Housing Benefit Regulations 2006 (exception to the benefit cap: receipt of specified benefit), after sub-paragraph (f) add–

"(g) the claimant is receiving universal credit.".

The Armed Forces and Reserve Forces Compensation Scheme (Consequential Provisions: Subordinate Legislation) Order 2013

(SI 2013 No.591)

Made	*12th March 2013*
Laid before Parliament	*15th March 2013*
Coming into force	*8th April 2013*

The Secretary of State, in exercise of the powers conferred by sections 1(2) and 10(2), (3) and (4) of the Armed Forces (Pensions and Compensation) Act 2004, makes the following Order:

Citation, commencement and interpretation

1. This Order may be cited as the Armed Forces and Reserve Forces Compensation Scheme (Consequential Provisions: Subordinate Legislation) Order 2013.

2. This Order comes into force as follows–

(1) Articles 1 to 7 come into force on 8th April 2013.

(2) Subject to paragraph (3), the Schedule comes into force on 8th April 2013.

(3) *[Omitted]*

Extent and application

3. Subject to articles 4, 5 and 6, this Order extends and applies to the United Kingdom.

4. The amendments made by paragraphs [...] 15 to 54 of the Schedule have the same extent and application as the provisions amended by those paragraphs.

5-6 *[Omitted]*

Consequential amendments and supplementary provisions

7. The Schedule has effect.

SCHEDULE

Article 7

Armed forces independence payments: consequential amendments and supplementary provisions

Amendment of the Social Security (Loss of Benefit) Regulations 2001

22.–(1) The Social Security (Loss of Benefit) Regulations 2001 are amended as follows.

(2) In regulation 1 (interpretation) at the appropriate place insert–

''armed forces independence payment" means armed forces independence payment under the Armed Forces and Reserve Forces (Compensation Scheme) Order 2011;".

(3)-(4) *[Omitted]*

Amendment of the Housing Benefit Regulations 2006

34.–(1) The Housing Benefit Regulations 2006 are amended as follows.

(2) In regulation 2(1)(interpretation)–

(a) at the appropriate place insert–

''armed forces independence payment'' means armed forces independence payment under the Armed Forces and Reserve Forces (Compensation Scheme) Order 2011;";

(b) In the paragraph defining "the benefit Acts" after "part 4 of the 2012 Act" insert '', the Armed Forces and Reserve Forces (Compensation Scheme) Order 2011";

(c) in the paragraph defining "person who requires overnight care''–

(i) omit "or" at the end of sub-paragraph (a)(iia);

(ii) after sub-paragraph (a)(iia) insert–

"(iib) is in receipt of armed forces independence payment; or"; and

(iii) in sub-paragraph (a)(iii) for ", (ii) or (iia)" substitute ", (ii), (iia) or (iib)".

(3) In regulation 28 (treatment of child care charges)–

(a) after paragraph (11)(d)(viii) insert–

"(ix) armed forces independence payment;";

(b) omit "or" after paragraph (13)(c); and

(c) after paragraph (13)(d) insert–

"; or

(e) in respect of whom armed forces independence payment is payable.".

(4) In regulation 74 (non-dependant deductions)–

(a) omit "or" after sub-paragraph (6)(b)(ii);

(b) after sub-paragraph (6)(b)(iii) insert–

"or

(iv) armed forces independence payment."; and

(c) in paragraph (9)(a) after "disability living allowance" insert ", armed forces independence payment".

(5) In regulation 79(6) (date on which change of circumstances is to take effect)–

(a) for "the Act or" substitute "the Act,"; and

(b) after "Part 4 of the 2012 Act" insert "or article 24A of the Armed Forces and Reserve Forces (Compensation Scheme) Order 2011".

(6) In Schedule 3 (applicable amounts)–

(a) in paragraph 7(2)–

(i) after "section 72(3) of the Act" for "or" insert ","; and

(ii) after "section 78(3) of the 2012 Act" insert "or armed forces independence payment";

(b) in paragraph 13(1)(a) (additional condition for the disability premium), in subparagraph (i), after "personal independence payment" insert ", armed forces independence payment,";

(c) in paragraph 14 (severe disability premium)–

(i) in sub-paragraph (2)(a)(i) after "section 78(3) of the 2012 Act" insert "or armed forces independence payment";

(ii) in sub-paragraph (2)(b)(i) after "section 78(3) of the 2012 Act" insert "or armed forces independence payment"; and

(iii) in sub-paragraph (4)(a) after "section 78(3) of the 2012 Act" insert "or armed forces independence payment";

(d) in paragraph 15 (enhanced disability premium)–

(i) after sub-paragraph (1)(c) insert–

"; or

(d) armed forces independence payment is payable in respect of (i) the claimant, or (ii) a member of the claimant's family, who has not attained the qualifying age for state pension credit,";

(e) in paragraph 16 (disabled child premium), after sub-paragraph (d) insert–

"; or

(e) is a young person who is in receipt of armed forces independence payment.".

(7) In Schedule 5 (sums to be disregarded in the calculation of income), in paragraph 6, after "disability living allowance" insert ", armed forces independence payment".

Amendment of the Housing Benefit (Persons who have attained the qualifying age for state pension credit) Regulations 2006

35.–(1) The Housing Benefit (Persons who have attained the qualifying age for state pension credit) Regulations 2006 are amended as follows.

(2) In regulation 2(1) (interpretation)–

(a) at the appropriate place insert–

"armed forces independence payment" means armed forces independence payment under the Armed Forces and Reserve Forces (Compensation Scheme) Order 2011;";

(b) in the definition of "the benefit Acts" after "part 4 of the 2012 Act" insert ", the Armed Forces and Reserve Forces (Compensation Scheme) Order 2011";
(c) in the definition of "person who requires overnight care"–
(i) omit "or" at the end of sub-paragraph (a)(iia);
(ii) after sub-paragraph (a)(iia) insert–

"(iib) is in receipt of armed forces independence payment; or"; and

(iii) in sub-paragraph (a)(iii) for ", (ii) or (iia)" substitute ", (ii), (iia) or (iib)".
(3) In regulation 29(1)(j)(i) (meaning of "income") after paragraph (1)(j)(ia) insert–

"(ib) armed forces independence payment;".

(4) In regulation 31 (treatment of child care charges)–
(a) after paragraph (11)(d)(viii) insert–

"(ix) armed forces independence payment;";

(b) after paragraph (13)(d) insert–

"; or
(e) in respect of whom armed forces independence payment is payable.".

(5) In regulation 55 (non-dependant deductions)–
(a) omit "or" after sub-paragraph (6)(b)(ii);
(b) after sub-paragraph (6)(b)(iii) insert–

"; or
(iv) armed forces independence payment,"; and

(c) in paragraph (10)(a) after "disability living allowance" insert ", armed forces independence payment".
(6) In regulation 59(6) (date on which change of circumstances is to take effect) after "Part 4 of the 2012 Act" insert "or the Armed Forces and Reserve Forces (Compensation Scheme) Order 2011".
(7) In Schedule 3 (applicable amounts)–
(a) in paragraph 5(2)–
(i) omit "or" after sub-paragraph (b); and
(ii) after sub-paragraph (c) insert–

"; or
(d) armed forces independence payment.";

(b) in paragraph 6 (severe disability premium)–
(i) in sub-paragraph (2)(a)(i) after "section 78(3) of the 2012 Act" insert "or armed forces independence payment";
(ii) in sub-paragraph (2)(b)(i) after "section 78(3) of the 2012 Act" insert "or armed forces independence payment";
(iii) in sub-paragraph (6)(a) after "section 78(3) of the 2012 Act" insert "or armed forces independence payment";
(c) in paragraph 7 (enhanced disability premium) after sub-paragraph (1)(b) insert–

"or
(c) armed forces independence payment is payable,";
(d) in paragraph 8 (disabled child premium) after sub-paragraph (d) insert–

"; or
(e) is a young person who is in receipt of armed forces independence payment.".

(8) In Schedule 4 (sums disregarded from claimant's earnings), in paragraph 5(1)(a)–
(a) omit "or" at the end of paragraph (viii); and
(b) after paragraph (viii) insert–

"(ix) armed forces independence payment; or".

(9) In Schedule 6 (capital to be disregarded), in paragraph 21(2), after paragraph (ba) insert–

"(bb) armed forces independence payment;".

Amendment of the Benefit Cap (Housing Benefit) Regulations 2012

48.–(1) The Benefit Cap (Housing Benefit) Regulations 2012 are amended as follows.

(2) In regulation 2(5)(amendment of the Housing Benefit Regulations 2006), in sub-paragraph (ea) of the inserted regulation 75F, after "personal independence payment" insert "or an armed forces independence payment under the Armed Forces and Reserve Forces (Compensation Scheme) Order 2011".

The Health and Social Care Act 2012 (Consequential Amendments) Order 2013

(SI 2013 No.594)

Made	*12th March 2013*
Coming into force	*1st April 2013*

The Secretary of State makes the following Order in exercise of the powers conferred by section
303 of the Health and Social Care Act 2012.
A draft of this Order has been laid before and approved by resolution of each House of Parliament
in accordance with section 304(5) of that Act.

Citation, commencement and extent

1.–(1) This Order may be cited as the Health and Social Care Act 2012 (Consequential Amendments) Order 2013.

(2) This Order comes into force on 1st April 2013.

---

(3)Any amendment made by this Order has the same extent as the provision amended. Amendment of the Welfare Reform Act 2012

7. In section 130(4)(a) of the Welfare Reform Act 2012 (information-sharing in relation to provision of overnight care etc), omit “a Primary Care Trust,”.

The Universal Credit (Consequential, Supplementary, Incidental and Miscellaneous Provisions) Regulations 2013

(SI 2013 No.630)

Made	*13th March 2013*
Laid before Parliament	*18th March 2013*
Coming into force	*29th April 2013*

The Secretary of State for Work and Pensions makes the following Regulations in exercise of the powers conferred by paragraph 5(4) of Schedule 1 to the Child Support Act 1991 (as it has effect apart from section 1 of the Child Support, Pensions and Social Security Act 2000), section 6J(2)(a) of the Jobseekers Act 1995 and sections 2(2), 4(6), 6(1) and (3), 26(2)(a), 32, 40, 42(1), (2) and (3) and 96(4)(c) of, and paragraph 4(3) of Schedule 1 to, the Welfare Reform Act 2012 ("the Act").

This instrument has not been referred to the Social Security Advisory Committee because it contains only regulations made under provisions of the Act, and provisions of the Child Support Act 1991 and of the Jobseekers Act 1995 inserted into those Acts by the Act, and is made before the end of the period of 6 months beginning with the coming into force of those provisions.

In accordance with section 176(2)(b) of the Social Security Administration Act 1992, the Secretary of State has obtained the agreement of organisations appearing to him to be representative of the authorities concerned that proposals in respect of these Regulations should not be referred to them.

PART 1
General

Citation, commencement, extent and application

1.–(1) These Regulations may be cited as the Universal Credit (Consequential, Supplementary, Incidental and Miscellaneous Provisions) Regulations 2013.

(2) These Regulations come into force on 29th April 2013.

(3) Subject to paragraphs (4) to (6), each of the amendments made by these Regulations has the same extent and application as the provision amended.

(4)-(6) *[Omitted]*

PART 2
Amendments of primary legislation

Amendment of the Welfare Reform and Pensions Act 1999

15. In section 72(3) of the Welfare Reform and Pensions Act 1999 (supply of information for certain purposes)–

(a) at the end of paragraph (c), delete "or"; and

(b) after paragraph (d) insert–

", or

(e) Part 1 of the Welfare Reform Act 2012.".

PART 3
Amendments of secondary legislation

CHAPTER 1
SOCIAL SECURITY BENEFITS

Amendment of the Housing Benefit Regulations 2006

35.–(1) The Housing Benefit Regulations 2006 are amended as follows.

(2) In regulation 2(1) (interpretation)–
(a) for the definition of "contributory employment and support allowance", substitute–

"contributory employment and support allowance" means an allowance under Part 1 of the Welfare Reform Act as amended by the provisions of Schedule 3, and Part 1 of Schedule 14, to the 2012 Act that remove references to an income-related allowance, and a contributory allowance under Part 1 of the Welfare Reform Act as that Part has effect apart from those provisions;"; and

(b) after the definition of "training allowance", insert–

"universal credit" means universal credit under Part 1 of the 2012 Act;".

(3) In regulation 19 (persons of a prescribed description), omit "or" after paragraph (2)(a) and after paragraph (2)(c) insert–

"; or
(d) entitled to an award of universal credit".

(4) In regulation 28(11) (treatment of child care charges), in sub-paragraphs (ba) and (ca), after "Employment and Support Allowance Regulations" insert "or the Employment and Support Allowance Regulations 2013(b)".

(5) In regulation 40(5A) (calculation of income other than earnings), after "Employment and Support Allowance Regulations" insert "or section 11J of the Welfare Reform Act".

(6) In regulation 56(2)(ea) (full-time students to be treated as not liable to make payments), after "Employment and Support Allowance Regulations" insert "or the Employment and Support Allowance Regulations 2013".

(7) In regulation 74 (non-dependant deductions)–
(a) for paragraph (8), substitute–

"(8) No deduction shall be made in calculating the amount of a rent rebate or allowance in respect of a non-dependant aged less than 25 who is–
(a) on income support, an income-based jobseeker's allowance or an income-related employment and support allowance which does not include an amount under section 4(2)(b) of the Welfare Reform Act (the support component and the work related activity component); or
(b) entitled to an award of universal credit where the award is calculated on the basis that the non-dependant does not have any earned income."; and

(b) after paragraph (10) insert–

"(11) For the purposes of paragraph (8), "earned income" has the meaning given in regulation 52 of the Universal Credit Regulations 2013.".

(8) In regulation 102(4) (method of recovery), after "Employment and Support Allowance Regulations" insert ", regulation 39(1)(a) of the Employment and Support Allowance Regulations 2013".

(9) In Schedule 3 (applicable amounts)–
(a) in Part 5 (the components), in paragraph 21(c)(ii), after "Employment and Support Allowance Regulations" insert "or regulation 7 of the Employment and Support Allowance Regulations 2013"; and
(b) in Part 7 (transitional addition)–
   (i) in paragraph 27(1)(b)(i), after "Employment and Support Allowance Regulations" insert "or regulation 26 of the Employment and Support Allowance Regulations 2013, in either case"; and

(ii) in paragraph 29(1)(c), after "Employment and Support Allowance Regulations" insert "or regulation 86 of the Employment and Support Allowance Regulations 2013".

(10) In Schedule 4 (sums to be disregarded in the calculation of earnings), paragraph 10A(6)(a), after "Employment and Support Allowance Regulations" insert "or regulation 39(1)(a), (b) or (c) of the Employment and Support Allowance Regulations 2013".

(11) In Schedule 5 (sums to be disregarded in the calculation of income other than earnings), in paragraph 7, after sub-paragraph (d) insert–

"(e) universal credit".

(12) In Schedule 6 (capital to be disregarded), in paragraph 9(1), after paragraph (f) insert–

"(g) universal credit,".

Amendment of the Housing Benefit (Persons who have attained the qualifying age for state pension credit) Regulations 2006

36.–(1) The Housing Benefit (Persons who have attained the qualifying age for state pension credit) Regulations 2006 are amended as follows.

(2) In regulation 2 (interpretation)–

(a) for the definition of "contributory employment and support allowance", substitute–

"contributory employment and support allowance" means an allowance under Part 1 of the Welfare Reform Act as amended by the provisions of Schedule 3, and Part 1 of Schedule 14, to the 2012 Act that remove references to an income-related allowance, and a contributory allowance under Part 1 of the Welfare Reform Act as that Part has effect apart from those provisions;"; and

(b) after the definition of "training allowance", insert–

" "universal credit" means universal credit under Part I of the 2012 Act;".

(3) In regulation 19 (persons of a prescribed description), omit "or" after paragraph (2)(a) and after paragraph (2)(c), insert–

"; or

(d) entitled to an award of universal credit".

(4) In regulation 31(11) (treatment of child care charges), in sub-paragraphs (ba) and (ca), after "Employment and Support Allowance Regulations" insert "or the Employment and Support Allowance Regulations 2013".

(5) In regulation 55 (non-dependant deductions)–

(a) in paragraph (8), after "work-related activity component)" insert "or who is entitled to an award of universal credit where the award is calculated on the basis that the person does not have any earned income"; and

(b) after paragraph (10) insert–

"(11) For the purposes of paragraph (8), "earned income" has the meaning given in regulation 52 of the Universal Credit Regulations 2013.".

(6) In regulation 83(4) (method of recovery), after "Employment and Support Allowance Regulations" insert ", regulation 39(1)(a) of the Employment and Support Allowance Regulations 2013".

(7) In Schedule 4 (sums disregarded from claimant's earnings)–

(a) in paragraph 5(1)(d)(ii), after "Employment and Support Allowance Regulations" insert "or regulation 7 of the Employment and Support Allowance Regulations 2013"; and

(b) in paragraph 5A(6)(a), after "Employment and Support Allowance Regulations" insert "or regulation 39(1)(a), (b) or (c) of the Employment and Support Allowance Regulations 2013".

(8) In Schedule 6 (capital to be disregarded), in paragraph 21(2), omit "or" after subparagraph (m) and after sub-paragraph (n) insert–

"; or

(o) universal credit".

The Housing Benefit (Amendment) Regulations 2013

(SI 2013 No.665)

Made	*19th March 2013*
Laid before Parliament	*21st March 2013*
Coming into force	*1st April 2013*

The Secretary of State for Work and Pensions makes the following Regulations in exercise of the powers conferred by sections 123(1)(d), 130A(2) to (5), 137(1) and (2)(h) and 175(1), (3) and (4) of the Social Security Contributions and Benefits Act 1992.

The Secretary of State has not referred proposals in respect of these Regulations to the Social Security Advisory Committee, as it appears to him that by reason of the urgency of the matter it is inexpedient to do so.

The Secretary of State has not undertaken consultation with organisations appearing to him to be representative of the authorities concerned, as it appears to him that by reason of the urgency of the matter it is inexpedient to do so.

Citation and commencement

1. These Regulations may be cited as the Housing Benefit (Amendment) Regulations 2013 and they come into force on 1st April 2013.

Amendment of the Housing Benefit Regulations 2006

2.–(1) The Housing Benefit Regulations 2006 are amended as follows.

(2) In regulation 2(1) (interpretation)–

(a) after the definition of "maximum rent (LHA)" insert–

"member of the armed forces away on operations" means a member of the regular forces or the reserve forces (within the meaning of section 374 of the Armed Forces Act 2006) who is absent, while on operations, from the dwelling usually occupied as their home;";

(b) after the definition of "qualifying income-related benefit" insert–

"qualifying parent or carer" means a person who has a bedroom in the dwelling they occupy as their home additional to those used by the persons who occupy the dwelling as their home and who–

(a) has a child or qualifying young person placed with them as mentioned in regulation 21(3) who by virtue of that provision is not treated as occupying their dwelling; or

(b) has been approved as a foster parent under regulation 27 of the Fostering Services (England) Regulations 2011 or regulation 28 of the Fostering Services (Wales) Regulations 2003 or as a kinship carer under regulation 10 or a foster carer under regulation 22 of the Looked After Children (Scotland) Regulations 2009 but does not have a child or qualifying young person placed with them and has not had a child or qualifying young person placed with them for a period which does not exceed 52 weeks;".

(3) In regulation B13 (determination of a maximum rent (social sector))–

(a) in paragraph (2)(b) for "paragraph (5)" substitute "paragraphs (5) to (7)";

(b) in paragraph (5) omit the words after sub-paragraph (e);

(c) after paragraph (5) add–

"(6) The claimant is entitled to one additional bedroom in any case where–

(a) the claimant or the claimant's partner is (or each of them is) a person who requires overnight care; or

(b) the claimant or the claimant's partner is (or each of them is) a qualifying parent or carer.

(7) The claimant is entitled to two additional bedrooms where paragraph (6)(a) and (b) both apply.

(8) For the purposes of determining the number of occupiers of the dwelling under paragraph (5), the relevant authority must include any member of the armed forces away on operations who–

(a) is the son, daughter, step-son or step-daughter of the claimant or the claimant's partner;

(b) was the claimant's non-dependant before they became a member of the armed forces away on operations; and

(c) intends to resume occupying the dwelling as their home when they cease to be a member of the armed forces away on operations.".

(4) In regulation 13D (determination of a maximum rent (LHA))–

(a) in paragraph (2)(c) for "paragraph (3)" substitute "paragraphs (3) to (3B)";

(b) in paragraph (3) omit the words after sub-paragraph (e);

(c) after paragraph (3) add–

"(3A) The claimant is entitled to one additional bedroom in any case where–

(a) the claimant or the claimant's partner is (or each of them is) a person who requires overnight care; or

(b) the claimant or the claimant's partner is (or each of them is) a qualifying parent or carer.

(3B) The claimant is entitled to two additional bedrooms where paragraph (3A)(a) and (b) both apply.";

(d) in paragraph (12) for the definition of "occupiers" substitute–

"occupiers" means–

(a) the persons whom the relevant authority is satisfied occupy as their home the dwelling to which the claim or award relates except for any joint tenant who is not a member of the claimant's household; and

(b) any member of the armed forces away on operations who–

(i) is the son, daughter, step-son or step-daughter of the claimant or the claimant's partner;

(ii) was the claimant's non-dependant before they became a member of the armed forces away on operations; and

(iii) intends to resume occupying the dwelling as their home when they cease to be a member of the armed forces away on operations;".

(5) In regulation 14(8) (requirement to refer to rent officers) in the definition of "change relating to a rent allowance" for "or (f)" substitute "(f) or (g)".

(6) In regulation 74 (non-dependant deductions) after paragraph (7)(f) add–

"(g) he is not residing with the claimant because he is a member of the armed forces away on operations.".

(7) In paragraph 2 of Schedule 2 (excluded tenancies)–

(a) in sub-paragraph (3) after paragraph (f) add–

"(g) the claimant or the claimant's partner becomes, or ceases to be, a qualifying parent or carer where that affects the size criteria, as set out in Schedule 2 to the Rent Officers Order, applicable in the claimant's case.";

(b) after sub-paragraph (3) add–

"(4) For the purposes of sub-paragraph (3)(d)(iii) it does not amount to a change in the composition of the household where a son, daughter, step-son or step-daughter of the claimant or the claimant's partner who is the claimant's non-dependant ceases to occupy the dwelling as their home because they become a member of the armed forces away on operations, or subsequently resumes occupying the dwelling as their home on ceasing to be a member of the armed forces away on operations.".

Amendment of the Housing Benefit (Persons who have attained the qualifying age for state pension credit) Regulations 2006

3.–(1) The Housing Benefit (Persons who have attained the qualifying age for state pension credit) Regulations 2006 are amended as follows.

(2) In regulation 2(1) (interpretation)–

(a) after the definition of "maximum rent (LHA)" insert–

"member of the armed forces away on operations" means a member of the regular forces or the reserve forces (within the meaning of section 374 of the Armed Forces Act 2006) who is absent, while on operations, from the dwelling usually occupied as their home;";

(b) after the definition of "qualifying income-related benefit" insert–

"qualifying parent or carer" means a person who has a bedroom in the dwelling they occupy as their home additional to those used by the persons who occupy the dwelling as their home and who–

(a) has a child or qualifying young person placed with them as mentioned in regulation 21(3) who by virtue of that provision is not treated as occupying their dwelling; or

(b) has been approved as a foster parent under regulation 27 of the Fostering Services (England) Regulations 2011 or regulation 28 of the Fostering Services (Wales) Regulations 2003 or as a kinship carer under regulation 10 or a foster carer under regulation 22 of the Looked After Children (Scotland) Regulations 2009 but does not have a child or qualifying young person placed with them and has not had a child or qualifying young person placed with them for a period which does not exceed 52 weeks;".

(3) In regulation 13D (determination of a maximum rent (LHA))–

(a) in paragraph (2)(c) for "paragraph (3)" substitute "paragraphs (3) to (3B)";

(b) in paragraph (3) omit the words after sub-paragraph (e);

(c) after paragraph (3) add–

"(3A) The claimant is entitled to one additional bedroom in any case where–

(a) the claimant or the claimant's partner is (or each of them is) a person who requires overnight care; or

(b) the claimant or the claimant's partner is (or each of them is) a qualifying parent or carer.

(3B) The claimant is entitled to two additional bedrooms where paragraphs (3A)(a) and (b) both apply.";

(d) in paragraph (12) for the definition of "occupiers" substitute–

"occupiers" means–

(a) the persons whom the relevant authority is satisfied occupy as their home the dwelling to which the claim or award relates except for any joint tenant who is not a member of the claimant's household; and

(b) any member of the armed forces away on operations who–
   (i) is the son, daughter, step-son or step-daughter of the claimant or the claimant's partner;
   (ii) was the claimant's non-dependant before they became a member of the armed forces away on operations; and
   (iii) intends to resume occupying the dwelling as their home when they cease to be a member of the armed forces away on operations;".

(4) In regulation 14(8) (requirement to refer to rent officers) in the definition of "change relating to a rent allowance" for "or (e)" substitute "(e) or (f)".

(5) In regulation 55 (non-dependant deductions) after paragraph (7)(f) add–

"(g) he is not residing with the claimant because he is a member of the armed forces away on operations.".

(6) In paragraph 2 of Schedule 2 (excluded tenancies)–

(a) in sub-paragraph (3) after paragraph (e) add–

"(f) the claimant or the claimant's partner becomes, or ceases to be, a qualifying parent or carer where that affects the size criteria, as set out in Schedule 2 to the Rent Officers Order, applicable in the claimant's case.";

(b) after sub-paragraph (3) add–

"(4) For the purposes of sub-paragraph (3)(d)(iii) it does not amount to a change in the composition of the household where a son, daughter, step-son or step-daughter of the claimant or the claimant's partner who is the claimant's non-dependant ceases to occupy the dwelling as their home because they become a member of the armed forces away on operations, or subsequently resumes occupying the dwelling as their home on ceasing to be a member of the armed forces away on operations.".

The Rent Officers (Housing Benefit Functions) Amendment Order 2013

(SI 2013 No.666)

Made	*19th March 2013*
Laid before Parliament	*21st March 2013*
Coming into force	*1st April 2013*

The Secretary of State for Work and Pensions makes the following Order in exercise of the powers conferred by section 122(1) and (6) of the Housing Act 1996.

Citation and commencement

1. This Order may be cited as the Rent Officers (Housing Benefit Functions) Amendment Order 2013 and comes into force on 1st April 2013.

Amendment of the Rent Officers (Housing Benefit Functions) Order 1997

2.–(1) The Rent Officers (Housing Benefit Functions) Order 1997 is amended as follows.

(2) In Schedule 2 (size criteria)–

(a) for paragraph 1A substitute–

"**1A.** One additional bedroom is allowed where on the application for the determination–

(a) the tenant or the tenant's partner is (or both of them are) stated as being a person who requires overnight care; or

(b) the tenant or the tenant's partner is (or both of them are) stated as being a qualifying parent or carer.

1B. Two additional bedrooms are allowed where sub-paragraphs (a) and (b) of paragraph 1A both apply.";

(b) after paragraph 2 add–

"**3.** In this Schedule "qualifying parent or carer" has the meaning given by regulation 2(1) of the Housing Benefit Regulations.".

Amendment of the Rent Officers (Housing Benefit Functions) (Scotland) Order 1997

3.–(1) The Rent Officers (Housing Benefit Functions) (Scotland) Order 1997 is amended as follows.

(2) In Schedule 2 (size criteria)–

(a) for paragraph 1A substitute–

"**1A.** One additional bedroom is allowed where on the application for the determination–

(a) the tenant or the tenant's partner is (or both of them are) stated as being a person who requires overnight care; or

(b) the tenant or the tenant's partner is (or both of them are) stated as being a qualifying parent or carer.

1B. Two additional bedrooms are allowed where sub-paragraphs (a) and (b) of paragraph 1A both apply.";

(b) after paragraph 2 add–

"**3.** In this Schedule "qualifying parent or carer" has the meaning given by regulation 2(1) of the Housing Benefit Regulations.".